"This wonderful engagement with the life of Joseph is the epitome of what it means in practice 'to apply thyself wholly to the text and to apply the text wholly to thyself.' Al Erisman illuminates the story in such a way that I felt I was traveling through life with Joseph—and what a life he lived! In the midst of each engagement with the text came a thought-provoking reflection on what this could mean for one who wants to live with vocational integrity today, both conceptually and specifically. Every chapter is an extraordinary combination of imagination, analysis, application, and profound wisdom. Regardless of one's age or circumstance in life, this book is worth reading and then reading again."

—Don Flow, Owner and CEO, Flow Automotive Companies, Winston-Salem, NC

"What a refreshing and inspiring book! Al Erisman does something that I would have thought impossible. He makes the ancient story of Joseph come alive with many wise insights for the kind of leadership much needed at Costco, Boeing, Microsoft, McDonald's—and the professional golf circuit! This book should be at the top of the reading lists for folks who care deeply about how faith in Christ can inform best practices of business leadership."

—Richard J. Mouw, PhD, President Emeritus and Professor of Faith and Public Life, Fuller Theological Seminary, Pasadena, CA

"Al has done an incredible job of presenting a very familiar story in a unique and inspiring way. Being the person others choose to follow. Providing inspiration. Behaving ethically. These are a few of the leadership characteristics you will learn about in *The Accidental Executive*. A must-read for leaders and potential leaders everywhere."

—Gloria S. Nelund, Chair and CEO, TriLinc Global Former CEO of Deutsche Bank North America Private Wealth Management, Manhattan Beach, CA

"*The Accidental Executive* made me see the Joseph story in a new light. The chapter 'When Bad Things Happen to Good People' is a good example. I found it helpful to be reminded that doing the right thing is not just a clever business strategy. It is a life choice that is often rewarded, but not always right away, and there are no guarantees."

—Jack vanHartesvelt, President, Hartland Hotel Company, Seattle, WA

"Al Erisman frames the life of Joseph like a polished MBA case study. With great care and intentionality, Erisman connects the dots and reveals the secret to what might seem to be an unlikely rise to power and fame. *The Accidental Executive* is wildly relevant and highly applicable to men and women of faith called to steward leadership roles in today's marketplace."

—Tami Heim, President and CEO of Christian Leadership Alliance, Nashville, TN; former Chief Publishing Officer, Thomas Nelson Publishers, Inc.

"I had the pleasure of working alongside Dr. Al Erisman at the Boeing Company. I was particularly moved by the preface as I had watched, from a distance, the incident with Al's fifth new boss in five years. His ultimate response to the incident—integrating his faith with his work—told me he was someone worth knowing. *The Accidental Executive* is worth getting to know as well."

—Scott Griffin, Boeing Vice President and Chief Information Officer (retired), Renton, WA

"A biblical story, which can be so easily dismissed as myth, in the hands of Al Erisman is transformed into a powerful guide for ethical business and life."

—Collin Timms, Chair, Guardian Bank, Bangalore, India

"Of the many books written in the life of Joseph, this one is distinguished by its practical perspective with real life examples used richly throughout. Al Erisman weaves his experience in the business world, and his keen understanding of Joseph's life, with the personal journeys of many to provide a tapestry of thought and instruction for the Christian executive. An easy but highly profitable read to see how God works in the business world for His glory and our edification."

—Bob Doll, Chief Equity Strategist, Nuveen Asset Management, New York City

"I have known Al Erisman for over ten years, and we have spoken on numerous occasions about our mutual admiration for Joseph. I'm so happy to see the book in its final copy. It is everything I had hoped it would be. This book will both admonish and encourage you in your faith walk and calling."

—Steven J. Bell, President and CEO, Bellmont Cabinet Co., Sumner, WA

"*The Accidental Executive* is a great addition to today's work and business literature. Al Erisman's study is truly a refreshing and unique contribution in following the gripping contours of the story of biblical patriarch Joseph throughout his stormy, 'accidental' career in Genesis. Al gives great personal examples from his own career at Boeing and from business leaders he has known—but he serves us most impressively by the way he allows Joseph's own experiences to challenge, inspire, and teach us."

—David W. Gill, PhD, Mockler-Phillips Professor of Workplace Theology & Business Ethics; Director, Mockler Center for Faith & Ethics in the Workplace, Gordon-Conwell Theological Seminary, South Hamilton, MA

"In this delightful and informative book, we see Joseph in a new light, a light that also illuminates our own practices of work and leadership. Al Erisman's insightful examination of the biblical text comes alive through fascinating stories from his own business experience and from dozens of interviews he conducted with executives. *The Accidental Executive* is a great read for any leader or aspiring leader who is looking for biblically based, practically shaped wisdom."

—Mark D. Roberts, PhD, Executive Director, Max De Pree Center for Leadership, Pasadena, CA

"This is the book to read if you want to see how a flesh-and-bone character from the Bible can generate practical insight for today's global businesses. Erisman knows the Bible, and his career as a Boeing technology executive, combined with his hundreds of interviews with leaders give him a brilliant perspective on business. *The Accidental Executive* is packed with high-impact examples of how spiritual growth, ethical integrity, and dynamic leadership like Joseph's can lead to business excellence today. It expanded my horizons about how much practical guidance the Bible has to give about my work."

—William Messenger, Executive Editor, Theology of Work Project, Boston, MA

"The story of Joseph was drawn to my attention as I was stepping into my appointment as CEO of the Singapore Exchange. It has inspired me through the years. Al has masterfully woven this ancient story into contemporary perspectives of business leadership."

—Hsieh Fu Hua, Cofounder and Adviser, PrimePartners Group, Singapore

"As a Christian in public service during a consequential time in America's history, Joseph's story really resonates with me. Finally, a fresh look at Joseph's life from the perspective of the business, work, and individual calling in addition to the traditional perspective of a person of faith. A must-read for anyone interested in finding greater meaning in their job."
—The Honorable Edmund C. Moy, 38th Director of the United States Mint, 2006–2011, Washington, DC

"Al Erisman is uniquely able to dig deep into the biblical story of Joseph and connect it to the lives and stories of business leaders in our day. Why? Because he's been a business leader himself and he's interviewed hundreds more. *The Accidental Executive* is personal, lively and enjoyable reading, and points us to the God of the Bible who cares about the work we do every day in service of the world he loves."
—Katherine Leary Alsdorf, Senior Fellow, Redeemer City to City Faith, Work & Leadership Initiative, New York City Board Member, Theology of Work Project

"Al Erisman brings us a fresh understanding of leadership lessons from the life of Joseph as he compares them to his own experiences and those of the many business and thought leaders he has interviewed over the last fifteen years. In so doing, he emphasizes the importance of integrating faith with work in a way that honors God. The reader will learn more of what it means to know God and be known by Him in both the joys and trials of life and work."
—C. William Pollard, Chairman Emeritus, The ServiceMaster Company, Wheaton, IL

"Why is it so hard for us to consistently view our work from a sacred perspective? *The Accidental Executive* uses the remarkable example of Joseph to help us lift up our view of work and to recognize God's purpose in it. Joseph's story, growing from slave to 'COO' in command of the largest kingdom of the day, will help you begin to see God's purpose for our professional lives and help you to bring meaning to your work."
—Bonnie Wurzbacher, Chief Resource Development Officer, World Vision International, London, UK; Sr. Vice President, Global Customer Leadership, The Coca-Cola Company (retired)

THE
ACCIDENTAL
EXECUTIVE

LESSONS ON BUSINESS, FAITH, AND CALLING
FROM THE LIFE OF JOSEPH

ALBERT M. ERISMAN

HENDRICKSON
PUBLISHERS

The Accidental Executive: Lessons on Business, Faith, and Calling from the Life of Joseph

© 2015 by Hendrickson Publishers Marketing, LLC
P. O. Box 3473
Peabody, Massachusetts 01961-3473

ISBN 978-1-61970-621-7

Unless otherwise noted, the Scripture quotations contained herein are taken from the Holy Bible, New International Version®, NIV®. Copyright © 1973, 1978, 1984, 2011 by Biblica, Inc.™ Used by permission of Zondervan. All rights reserved worldwide. www.zondervan.com The "NIV" and "New International Version" are trademarks registered in the United States Patent and Trademark Office by Biblica, Inc.™

Kind permission granted by Seattle Pacific University and the Institute for Business, Technology, and Ethics for the use of *Ethix* interview material.

Printed in the United States of America

First Printing—May 2015

Library of Congress Cataloging in Publication Data

Erisman, A. M.
    The accidental executive : lessons on business, faith, and calling
from the life of Joseph / Albert M. Erisman.
      pages cm
    Includes bibliographical references and index.
    ISBN 978-1-61970-621-7 (alk. paper)
    1. Joseph, Son of Jacob. 2. Leadership—Religious aspects—
Christianity. 3. Business—Religious aspects—Christianity. I. Title.
    BS580.J6E75 2015
    222'.11092—dc23
                2014048564

CONTENTS

PREFACE

It was the worst day of my thirty-two-year Boeing career.

It was December 1987 when Joe, my fifth new boss in five years, told me that starting in the New Year, I and my applied research team (about 180 people) would no longer report to him but to one of my colleagues in the organization. In short, I was being demoted. Further, the person to whom I would report was in the operations area and had no appreciation for the research we did. My other activity with the senior management of the company would cease. I was uninvited to the big gathering with the executives of our division in Florida the next March. My career had come to a screeching halt.

Although this happens every day in big business, it was the context of this move that was so troubling. Let me back up a bit to fill out the story.

My organization was in the computing division of the company, supporting both internal Boeing colleagues and external clients through the computer services sales division. Boeing had recently acquired a Cray supercomputer, the most powerful computer in the world at that time. A very small portion of the work our research staff did was to understand how to make use of this powerful computer. In addition to Boeing using this computer, oil companies wanted to try it out. Working through the sales organization, the manager of our applied mathematics group and I made monthly, sometimes weekly, trips to the oil country in Texas and Oklahoma to explain the power and potential of this supercomputer. As the oil companies signed up to use our Cray, it wasn't long before there was a satellite dish streaming data into our supercomputer. Because of this, Joe, the sales manager from the oil region, became the leader in revenue generation for the computer services division, and he gained company-wide recognition. We even nominated Joe to go to an executive graduate program to prepare him for a fast-track executive career. Joe's first new assignment after returning from his year away was to be my boss, and my demotion was one of his first actions.

I did not handle the news of the new assignment well. It was difficult to go back and explain the new organizational alignment to my staff and ultimately the 180 people in our applied research group, most of whose work had nothing to do with our super-computer. Those most directly involved in supporting Joe in his previous assignment, recommending him for the fast track, and now working for him under these new conditions, were outraged.

About a month into this difficult period, I had a call from a head hunter pointing me to a position in another part of the country. After an interview trip, I was offered the position of CEO of a small software company in the Midwest, and my wife and I took a trip to look at housing possibilities. We were living in the Seattle area at the time. Ultimately, we decided to say no to the opportunity.

Back then, I could not have told you why we made that decision. I remember that my wife and I told God that we would go if he wanted us to go, and stay if he wanted us to stay. But it seemed that we heard only silence. In retrospect, I did hear from God through the counsel of my pastor, Mark, who advised me to stay. It turned out to be the right decision for our family at the time, but I had hoped for a thunderclap response directly from God—and didn't get one.

Making the decision to stay did help my own attitude and leadership, and I tried hard to refocus our research group. We still had customers to serve, creative work to do, and we had an innovative passion that wasn't stopped by the "bump in the road." We did accomplish some good things that difficult year, in spite of seeing almost 25 percent of the highly qualified researchers in the organization decide to leave the company.

About November 1988, two things coincided. First, Joe was "reassigned" to another place in the company and never reentered the fast track. Orv, an executive for whom I had worked earlier in my career, replaced Joe's boss. I had a good relationship with Orv and I trusted him. Second, I heard a sermon on Joseph from Pastor Mark.

I set up an appointment with Orv early that next week and did something unlike anything I had ever done at Boeing (please note that I do not recommend this approach to others!). I told him the following:

> On Sunday I heard a sermon on Joseph from the Bible. Joseph, through no fault of his own, found himself sold into slavery, falsely accused by his boss, and put in prison. While he was in prison he did two things. First, he worked hard and honorably. He was appointed to be in charge of all of the other prisoners and was completely trusted by the jailer. Second, even while he did this, he never missed an opportunity to send a message out of prison stating that he was there because he was falsely accused, and he wanted out. Orv, we are in prison. We are here for no good reason. During this past year, we have worked very hard, and here is a summary of some of the good things our people have accomplished for the company. But we have lost 25 percent of the organization, we are struggling to recruit good people to fill in, and this is hurting not just us but also The Boeing Company. Could you do something about it?

To my surprise (which shows my own lack of faith), he promised to look into it. Two weeks later, he announced a reorganization in which our team would report to a supportive executive. That turned the tide for all of us. Orv never stopped calling me "Preacher" after that, but it changed my own life and the lives of the people in the organization. It established the first link for me between my business career and the story of Joseph.

There are lots of ways to look at the story of Joseph, but that very personal incident in my own life started me looking at him as a worker and as a businessperson. As I reread the story in Genesis, I saw how the events of his life prepared him for a position of leadership, how he dealt with success as well as failure, how he worked hard regardless of his circumstances, how he created a strategy and executed that strategy, how he dealt with temptations, and how he gained perspective on the purpose and meaning of his work. That study became the basis for this book.

I was raised on Bible stories, hearing them at home and church from as long ago as I can remember. Before I was five years old, I could have told you many stories about Jesus, David, Joseph, Daniel, Esther, and Ruth. A friend and mentor, Albert E. Greene, later taught me that we can see these stories through many different lenses, and each view provides a new insight for us. It was Al who encouraged me to take this nontraditional look at the story of Joseph.

In 1998, my colleague David Gill and I began to publish *Ethix* magazine. For eleven years, this was a bimonthly print magazine, while it now continues online (www.ethix.com). Each edition of *Ethix* includes a conversation with a leader, focusing on insight for making tough decisions in twenty-first-century business. I have now conducted over one hundred such interviews with leaders from many parts of the world. They include CEOs and presidents of *Fortune* 100 companies, owners of innovative small businesses, and leaders from government, education, and the academic world. Although there is a gap of about thirty-five hundred years between Joseph and these twenty-first-century business leaders, I am amazed at the strong parallels. I will share quotes from these interviews in places where their experience connects with the story of Joseph.

In 2001, I left Boeing and began teaching in the School of Business and Economics at Seattle Pacific University in Washington, and in 2006, I was involved in a project to start a microfinance program in the Central African Republic. I have taught on small business in many developing countries in the world, and I am on the board of three startup companies, two of them begun by former students. Out of these experiences, I created and taught a course called "Introduction to Business" for undergraduates at SPU, trying to help students gain an appreciation for what it takes to start and run a business. These experiences provide a perspective on business that is complementary to my time at Boeing, a large multinational corporation, and create a more diverse business backdrop for this book.

Though the development of this book started with a single incident at Boeing more than twenty-five years ago, many other threads have gone into this work. I am grateful for the opportunity to share it with you.

Al Erisman
Bellevue, Washington

INTRODUCTION

Business in the twenty-first century is fast paced, global, and rooted in technology. We like to think that we are at the high point of progress, and that our society, designs, and ideas are way ahead of past cultures. We think that there is not a great deal we can learn about business from history, with the possible exception of mistakes or failures to avoid.

But then we confront the Pyramids. How did a primitive society accomplish such an architectural feat? Consider Machu Picchu, the ancient Peruvian city built by the Incan civilization in the fifteenth century. Or see the ruins of ancient Roman civilization. We think of the Hanging Gardens of Babylon, one of the seven wonders of the ancient world. Or we visit Stonehenge. How were those "primitive" people able to create such beauty, such magnificent designs, without our design technology and our powerful machines?

Maybe we are not at the zenith of progress after all.

Surely, however, ancient civilizations couldn't tell us anything about how to run a multinational corporation. We couldn't learn from the past about how to lay out a strategy, execute that strategy responding to changes in the environment, or deal with leadership challenges that come both from success and failure. After all, there were no MBA programs, no Harvard, and no market systems to facilitate success. Surely, we can't learn about finding purpose and meaning in our work from business stories of an ancient civilization.

But we can.

Even if we are humbled by the design and organizational/ leadership capabilities of the past, however, we must acknowledge that today's tools for business, particularly technology, are a modern invention. Instantaneous access to information and ideas globally has created changes in business that we are still coming to understand and use. Surely, this aspect of business is new. Perhaps. But while technology creates many new ways of competing in business in the twenty-first century, it does not replace fundamentals. Great products, delivery, strategy, execution, markets, meeting needs, customer service, and so on are all common to businesses—new and old. The "dot coms" gave us technology without business fundamentals, which should teach us that the basics still matter. We should be willing to set aside some of the modern particulars and relearn lessons for business from great success stories of the past.

In this spirit, we will look at the life of Joseph—son of Jacob, son of Isaac, son of Abraham—whose story is told in the Bible in Genesis 37–50. Joseph is an intriguing character from many points of view, and much has been written about him. There are scores of books dealing with his faithfulness to God in difficult circumstances, the challenge of his upbringing as the favorite son of his father Jacob and all of the jealousy and rivalry that created, and his dreams. Andrew Lloyd Webber's musical (and subsequent movie) *Joseph and the Amazing Technicolor Dreamcoat* has made Joseph a popular and widely known figure, even among those who have never read the Bible.

But I want to approach this story from a different angle. Joseph had two phases of his career that offer insight for any modern-day person. In the first phase, he worked at the bottom of the organization, as a slave and a prisoner. He had little choice in his assignment; he could only choose how he would carry it out. His work was much like that of so many today. In the second phase of his career, Joseph accomplished a major feat that would challenge the best businessperson of modern times. He identified a problem, created a solution, and implemented that solution on a grand scale. He was the leader of a large organization. Through his work, he saved his civilization from starvation, enabling the world to survive a great famine in Egypt. In short, he created a strategy for a global business that had an impact on the world, not unlike what Microsoft or Boeing has done today. When we look at Joseph's story through this lens, we can gain insight about top leadership in business today.

There are three levels of insight that come from looking at the life of Joseph this way. At one level, we can learn from the story of Joseph about moral questions related to our work. How can we deal with temptation and the trifecta of money, sex, and power? How can we deal with the unique challenges that come to any businessperson, which require courage when things are difficult and the wisdom to handle success when things are going well?

It is important not to overlook the challenges Joseph faced in the early years of his career at the bottom of the organization chart. Many people have no opportunity to choose their own careers. They live their lives as "wage slaves," just trying to get by. Joseph found himself in this position for the same two reasons we do today: through errors of judgment that got him into trouble, and through circumstances beyond his control.

It is equally important not to miss how Joseph dealt with his success. We have only to read the headlines of the newspapers today to see business leaders who have fallen, not for lack of expertise, but for character flaws. They give in to sexual temptation. They focus on their own wealth, ultimately convincing themselves that they, as leaders, are above the law. They harbor bitterness and envy that change a motivating force into a destructive force. And when confronted with great difficulty that may come from events outside their control, they lose heart or retreat to salvaging their own position. If we are honest, then we recognize we are also vulnerable to these temptations, both at times of difficulty and at times of success.

Dealing with success may look out of place on a list of moral challenges, but I have observed that some leaders do very well in times of difficulty only to stumble and fall when things appear to be going great. Perhaps it is because they were dependent on God in the difficult times, but then when things were going well they somehow convinced themselves that their success was all of their own making. They feel self-confident, almost arrogant, and forget to be watchful. I have certainly seen these tendencies in my own life. Most churches offer special prayers for people in times of difficulty, whether they are dealing with health issues, the loss of a job, or other personal challenges. But perhaps it would be wise to offer special prayers for people who are doing well! We will see how Joseph protected himself from failure due to his success.

A second level is to examine the story of Joseph for insight into the technical aspects of business: leadership, planning, execution, and globalization. In fact, business schools focus a great deal on these areas, and we can easily regard these as tools that have little connection to faith or a spiritual dimension. But I am reminded of the words of Abraham Kuyper (1837–1920) from a speech he gave at his opening address at the Free University in Amsterdam in 1880: "There is not a square inch in the whole domain of our human existence over which Christ, who is Sovereign over all, does not cry: Mine!" We may not expect to gain insight into such technical aspects by looking at Scripture, but these are also a part of the biblical story.

Business schools tend to put a great deal more emphasis on strategy than execution. Look at the business section of your local bookstore and you will likely see at least ten books on strategy for every book on execution, yet it is in execution that the business succeeds or fails. In execution, leaders must respond to a changing world that is different from the world identified in the planning scenarios, and they must deal with it in real time. Joseph encountered all of these issues in running his business. We will see that these tools are not simply neutral—to be applied without thought or connection to the impact they have on the people of the organization—but that they have a moral weight as well.

At the third level, we will see that Joseph's story offers good insight into the big questions for people in business: finding a career, seeing meaning in our work, and building the bridge between our faith and our work. Today, for many people of faith, there remains a gap between Sunday and Monday, between the importance of our worship and study of the Scriptures, and the day-to-day decisions we need to make in our business life Monday through Friday. The idea that there is one kind of behavior appropriate for business and another type for home just doesn't work, and the attempt to segment life in this way is at the heart of so many business failures.

Why is this? I believe that acting with integrity is indispensable for any good business leader. But what I mean by integrity is a bit different from the meaning often attached to the word. For many, integrity is simply honesty, doing what you say you will do, telling the truth. While it certainly includes these, I think the full meaning of integrity is so much more. Integrity means wholeness. From the same root word we get *integer*, which refers to whole numbers, and *integration*, which means "bringing things together into one." Wholeness is the key for a business leader as well. Living the same life at work as at home avoids the problem of leaving values at home when the leader goes to work. Integrity doesn't allow people of faith to leave that faith, that call on their lives, outside the door of the office. Gaining wholeness, we will find, was vital for Joseph—and it is vital for us.

Interestingly, it is our modern, technologically infused world that is helping us to see clearly how important this wholeness, this integrity, truly is. Business in the twenty-first century has become 24/7 for many people in this technologically connected world, limiting our ability to isolate it into the Monday-through-Friday realm.

Living and working in a 24/7 world is both a challenge and an opportunity. The challenge is that our work can consume us to the point of neglecting our family, health, and spiritual development. The opportunity is that since we cannot segment our lives into our Sunday self and our Monday self, we can bring our whole selves to work: our values, our purpose, and our faith. We even find that it is in this world of work that we put into practice the spiritual disciplines learned on Sunday. Neglecting this connection leads to spiritual weakness. For some people, this integration of work and faith is limited to sharing their faith or, at most, acting ethically in their business. But Joseph's story will help us see that our faith has much more to do with business than we have been taught.

In developing this business account of Joseph's life, I have chosen to follow the events of the story as they appear in the Bible, taking the insight as it comes. I am assuming the reader is familiar with the general flow of the story. For those who are not, it would be a simple matter to read it in the Bible in Genesis 37–50. For the part about his education, rooted in the career of his father Jacob, read Genesis 25–35. I will summarize key points of the stories as we draw from them.

The question of dreams is one aspect of this story that many twenty-first-century readers may find problematic. In four different places, we find the interpretation of a dream to be a central element of the account. While we have gained more scientific understanding of the brain and of dreams since Joseph's time, even now we are not certain about dreams. How do we regard an ancient civilization where dreams were used to tell the future? Perhaps in that earlier civilization, without books or communications systems, God used dreams as a means of communicating his intent to people. Similarly, Joseph's ability to interpret dreams could be God's expression of commitment to working with Joseph in a special way. Others have tried to explain some other way that Joseph might have drawn meaning from the dreams he either had or was told. I don't know the answer to this.

Starting with Joseph's own dreams, followed by the dreams of the chief cupbearer and the chief baker (both while in prison), and culminating with the dreams of Pharaoh, we see dreams foretelling real events when seen through Joseph's interpretation. Rather than trying to develop a theory for the role of dreams and their interpretation in an ancient land, I will simply take the insight that comes from interpreting this story from a business perspective and leave the analysis to others.

But another way of thinking about Joseph's dreams is the other way we often use the word. We all have dreams about the future, including what we will do and how we will do it. These dreams give us hope. We will therefore consider this aspect of his dreams as well.

Near the end of the story, Joseph reflects on the purpose of what he was called to do, and this brings us to see the role of purpose and meaning in our own lives in business. Did things work out exactly the way we think they should? And if not, what can we learn from the outcomes that were not so favorable?

There are many things about the story of Joseph that are not told in Genesis. I wonder how he managed his team, what doubts he may have had along the way, and why he made some of the choices he made. Sometimes I have drawn inferences, but I have tried to stay with what we know from the biblical account. In the final chapter, I have collected a set of questions I would like to ask Joseph.

Finally, we should recognize that Joseph was a real person, not a caricature. He had great strengths, but he also had weaknesses. We need to consider both as we try to learn about business from a gifted, but not perfect, business leader.

Along the way, my own experience in business and the interviews I conducted with business leaders will find their way into the story as well. We will find that the thirty-five-hundred-year gap is not as great as it first appears, and this business view of Joseph really does have something to say to us in the twenty-first century.

1

EDUCATION

Joseph is introduced to us by name for the first time in Genesis 30. But we don't hear any more about him until he reaches age seventeen in Genesis 37. Since there was no developed university system in that day, children learned from their fathers about life and work, which meant that Joseph's early formal education came from his father Jacob. Education plays an important shaping role in the life of any leader, so to understand the nature of this education and what he might have learned, we need to gain insight into the character and work of Jacob. As with so many leaders today, Joseph's teacher is neither a hero nor a villain, but a complex mix of great insight and bad judgment.

Jacob, son of Isaac, is one of the first great businesspeople we encounter in the Bible. He fits the stereotype many people have for business leaders: smart, scheming, always looking for an angle. No one, friend or foe, would get in the way of a business deal. Even his name means deceiver. When we first meet Jacob, his older twin brother Esau has come in from working in the fields and is famished. Jacob has just made a pot of red stew and offers some to Esau in exchange for his birthright, which included all of the benefits that went to the eldest son in those days. Later, when their father Isaac is about to die, Jacob and his mother scheme together to trick Isaac into blessing Jacob rather than Esau—which he does. Esau then seeks revenge, and Jacob has to escape for his life. His mother suggests he go and stay for a while with Laban, her brother, in a distant country. But along the way, Jacob has an encounter with God. This encounter changes him in some ways, but the schemer remains.

While with Laban, Jacob fell in love with Rachel, one of Laban's daughters. Though Laban promised Jacob he could have Rachel as his wife in exchange for seven years of work for him, Laban did not act with honor. He tricked Jacob into marrying his older daughter Leah. After discovering this, Jacob was also given Rachel as his wife a week later, but had to commit to another seven years of labor for Laban. Before he could leave with his family, Jacob was convinced to work additional time, twenty years in all. Not to be outdone, Jacob found a way to gain ownership of much of Laban's wealth over the final years through creative deal-making. With mounting tension between Jacob and Laban over the "transfer of wealth," Jacob finally gathered the huge flocks and herds he had collected, and escaped back to his father's land (Genesis 30–31), taking with him his various wives and eleven sons, including Joseph.

On the way home, Jacob met up with his brother Esau and feared for his life because of his past trickery. He again had an encounter with God and gained a blessing from God in the process. Jacob was able to hear a reiteration of the promise made to his father Isaac and grandfather Abraham, that all nations of the earth would be blessed through his family. Acknowledging that God had blessed him with great wealth, he offered Esau a settlement. After all of these years, Esau's anger had subsided, and Jacob was able to resettle in his father's territory (Genesis 32–33). Rachel gave birth to Benjamin, her second son, Jacob's twelfth, but she died in childbirth (Genesis 35). As we shall see, Benjamin plays a key role in the story of Joseph.

Jacob was one of the first great businessmen. When Milton Friedman said the purpose of business is to make as much money as you can, he could have used Jacob as his model. His brother, his father, and his uncle could not get in his way. But he was obviously more than simply a ruthless deal-maker. He had that knack of seeing a deal and having it work out—he possessed a combination of skill and good fortune we often associate with sharp, successful businesspeople. Had he lived today, we would likely say that he had the Midas touch.

But he had another "calling" as well. His encounters with God made him realize that he was in a particular position of privilege and responsibility, and he promised to give back to God 10 percent of his earnings. God had spoken, not just to him but to his father Isaac and his grandfather Abraham, about the role he and his family would play on this earth. God had said to Isaac, "I will be with you and will bless you. . . . I will make your descendants as numerous as the stars in the sky and will give them all these lands, and through your offspring all nations on earth will be blessed" (Genesis 26:3–4). Like his father, Jacob was to be a witness of God for the blessing of others. Had Jacob lived today, we would likely say he had the role of a missionary, bringing the blessings of God to the world.

How did these callings link together? Jacob acknowledged God in his work. In Genesis 31 he made the decision to leave Laban and return home after listening to God. He attributed the accumulation of his wealth to God and asked God to come to his aid and preserve that wealth when he was about to encounter his brother Esau (Genesis 32). But there is no mention of God in the process of his work and the way he went about accumulating his wealth and negotiating his deals. His business world operated by a different set of rules from those of his spiritual world. In modern-day language, we would say he had a dualistic worldview. Living by two sets of rules violates integrity, or wholeness, and his life makes this clear as we go forward in the story. God changed his name to Israel ("he who struggles with God"), and I wonder if this was a part of that struggle.

Most of us can probably identify with Jacob's mentality. As a much younger person, when I started my business career at Boeing, I had a strong faith commitment and a commitment to business that even I did not understand at the time. These different lives met in two ways. I did pledge to give 10 percent of my earnings to the work of God, and people around me knew of my Christian commitment. I tried to carry out my work in a way that demonstrated sound ethics, but the idea that the connection between faith and work could go deeper than that was foreign to me. It took some other influences in my life to learn what else this connection might look like.

In 1980, I heard a radio interview with Wayne Alderson, a Christian and a former steel company executive, whose life is the subject of the book *Stronger than Steel* by R. C. Sproul (New York: Harper and Row, 1980). Wayne saw his work in the steel business as a calling from God. It influenced the way he did his job, how he built connections between labor and management in an otherwise rancorous environment, and how this work ultimately affected the bottom line of the company. I bought the book on the way home from work that day, read it all the way through that night, and called Wayne the next day. It took a bit of work to track down his number, but when we connected we talked for an hour and we became friends. The insights he shared about making the connection between work and faith greatly affected my life (you will hear more about Wayne later). He provided a model for me, demonstrating how the connection between work and faith could be so much stronger than the one Jacob modeled. The concept of the dualistic life that Jacob so well characterized continues to this day. For many of us, the link between our faith and our work is weak at best. Often this is something we have simply not thought much about.

A second insight we can gain from the life of Jacob deals with the intrinsic importance of his work. He fully acknowledged that the wealth from his work came from God, but he seems to have treated his work simply as the means to that wealth. There is no evidence, and plenty of counterevidence, that he saw value from the work itself and could use that work to bless those around him, as God had said to him in Genesis 28.

We will see that Joseph stands in sharp contrast to his father in these two ways. He did see the process of his work as a gift from God, seeking God in the insight he brought to his work. In addition, the work itself had meaning, and through it he was able to demonstrate the love of God to those around him.

Education is a foundational element for any career. Some parents believe it is important for their children to get into the right preschool so they can get into the right kindergarten, allowing them to get into the right prep school, and ultimately into the right university. Education is important, but not in the way I just described.

Joseph is one example of a leader with an unorthodox education, but there are many modern examples. Jack Welch (General Electric) did not go to an Ivy League school but to Fairfield University. He said it provided a great education but also drove him to work harder to compete with his Ivy League colleagues. Alan Mulally (Ford) received his degree in engineering from the University of Kansas. Steve Jobs (Apple) and Bill Gates (Microsoft) both dropped out of college. Bonnie Wurzbacher (vice president at Coca-Cola) and Gloria Nelund (president, Deutsche Bank Capital Assets and CEO of TriLinc Global) both received elementary teaching degrees from small colleges. Many, many more examples could be included. None suggest education is unimportant, but all help us see that formal education is only one part of the education process.

Usually some aspect of formal education becomes a foundation for later learning upon which a career is built. For Steve Jobs, it was a calligraphy class he audited at Reed College before he dropped out. His lifelong passion for artistic beauty started here and shaped everything about Apple as a company. Gloria Nelund found out when she began student teaching what she *didn't* want to do and instead took an entry-level job in a bank. Discovering her passion for finance happened along the way, which she developed through a return to education at the Wharton School. So although we should expect that Joseph's life would be shaped by his early training, we should also remember that education is a lifelong journey. A good formal education prepares a person to learn the rest of their lives. Yet graduating from college, or completing another kind of formal education, is not the end but the beginning.

Still another shaping influence for most people is their early developmental environment. For example, Steve Jobs, the iconic Apple founder, was adopted as a child. That circumstance strongly affected the destructive way he related to others in his workplace, according to biographer Walter Isaacson.

It is interesting to note that Scripture introduces the story of Joseph with the words, "This is the account of Jacob's family line" (Genesis 37:2). As every person is shaped by the early influences of their lives, we can expect to see a young man develop in his father's image. Ultimately, early influences mix with personal character and life circumstances to create a unique individual, more than a replica of the teacher. We don't know what other influences were present that caused Joseph to follow a different path. Certainly his relationship with God was part of this. Perhaps his mother made a difference. Though it didn't happen all at once, we see Joseph grow in maturity and develop an integrated lifestyle that allowed him to live the same way with his work and his family, both under God. But not at the beginning.

2

READY?

When we first encounter Joseph in Genesis 37, he is seventeen years old. The favoritism his father showed him, likely as a result of being Jacob's beloved Rachel's first son, was evident to all. The Scripture mentions the problem in two ways: it tells us that his father made him a richly ornamented robe (Genesis 37:3), and that Joseph brought "a bad report" about his brothers and their work (Genesis 37:2). We don't know the nature of his brothers' offenses, but we do know that reporting this in a straightforward way could not have endeared Joseph to his brothers. Their reaction to him is clear: "When his brothers saw that their father loved him more than any of them, they hated him and could not speak a kind word to him" (Genesis 37:4).

This is enough dysfunction in a home to make it difficult for even a mature person to navigate the political waters. It may be that these experiences helped Joseph later in navigating the politics of Pharaoh's organization, but for now it was not a pretty sight.

And then he poured gasoline on the fire. He had a dream, and immediately he said to his brothers, " 'Listen to this dream I had: We were binding sheaves of grain out in the field when suddenly my sheaf rose and stood upright, while your sheaves gathered around mine and bowed down to it.' . . . And [his brothers] hated him all the more because of his dream and what he had said" (Genesis 37:8).

He didn't learn. "Then he had another dream, and he told it to his brothers. 'Listen,' he said, 'I had another dream, and this time the sun and moon and eleven stars were bowing down to me'" (Genesis 37:9). As a result, "his brothers were jealous of him, but his father kept the matter in mind" (Genesis 37:11).

Joseph had several things working against him at this point. He was a favorite of his father, something he could not control but seemed to enjoy; he was a snitch; and he talked about his two dreams, not learning from the bad reaction to the first when he told the second. Thinking about the context, he would probably have been wise to keep at least the interpretation to himself. It is easy to see him as arrogant here. And it is easy to see why his brothers were jealous and angry.

But I am going to be a bit more kind to Joseph. I see him as someone who is too young to play the game of thinking about the right thing to say, and simply said what was on his mind. In many ways, this is why I enjoy teaching university freshmen. They often express what they know in a way so straightforward that I wonder if they are aware of the impact of what they are saying.

I can relate to Joseph's early immaturity, although I think I also had a good work ethic at his age. When I came to my first full winter in Chicago at age eleven, I discovered a job opportunity that didn't exist in my old home city in California: shoveling snow. In the winter of 1952 I discovered that by grabbing a snow shovel and walking through the neighborhood offering my services for a fee, I could make quite a lot of money—but I learned early on that it wasn't just about the money. I remember one winter evening when I had finished shoveling a neighbor's walk, and before I went to the door to collect the agreed-upon fee, how I stood there admiring my work. Snow covered everything, the street light shone down, and there was a neat and clean path through the snow. I had learned something about the intrinsic value of work. From there I had lawn-mowing jobs and a paper route, and I continued shoveling snow in the winters until I turned sixteen and could get my first "real job" in an office.

But in many ways, like Joseph, I was immature. One night, when I started my snow shoveling work, we had a foot of new snow and I was out working the neighborhood. I came to one house with a long driveway, a walk parallel to the street, and a walk to a large uncovered porch. I agreed to do the whole thing for five dollars, a lot of money in those days. When I started working I discovered that the snow was light as a feather. What I thought would take me an hour of hard work I completed in ten minutes with barely a flake left on any concrete surface. When I went to collect my money, the homeowner said, "How could you have done it so quickly? That is more than I would make at my office for that much time." I responded, "There are lots of houses I won't be able to get to. Grab a shovel and get to work." His glare told me he was not amused. I also remember my father asking me to shovel the walk at our home, but I cheekily replied, "Paying customers first." I lacked the maturity to talk appropriately with my elders. I didn't even think about the fact that my father had purchased the shovel I used until many years later.

Our first job, and the attitude with which we approach it, is often the foundational element for a career. Gloria Nelund is co-founder and chairperson of TriLinc Global, an international investment fund. She came to this position after spending a number of years as president of Deutsche Bank's capital assets management group. In our interview, I learned that she had never even intended to go into finance. She was trained as a teacher but found out in her senior year of college that she didn't want to teach. So she found an entry-level position in a local bank, doing clerical work in its trust department. When a person was holding a number of shares of a particular stock and wanted to sell some of them, her job was to receive the certificate, stamp it closed, and create two new certificates, one for the buyer and the other representing the remaining shares for the seller. Then she entered the data on file cards. All of this was done with a typewriter! But here is the interesting thing about the way she approached that job.

I found that this was kind of fun. I loved understanding the financial world and just kept taking on new tasks to learn more. Early in my career, I adopted three principles that I would follow all of my life. I would work really hard, I would solve problems, and I would help people. The first meant that when I finished an assignment I would look for another one. I was always asking for more to do. It was much later in my career when I realized that not everybody did that![1]

If you were not a hard worker, I imagine it must have been difficult to work with Gloria. Rather than slowly completing each task to fill the time, she asked for more work when she was done. Gloria offered something that Joseph did not, at least at this point: she helped people, and she found that she enjoyed it. But those co-workers who wanted to work less may well have felt threatened by Gloria in the same way that Joseph's brothers, who had already shown themselves to be hot-tempered and devious, felt threatened by him.

Not long after this, Gloria was promoted to run the whole department. Joseph was given an important assignment by his father as well. But Gloria, as we shall see, was ready for her leadership assignment, while Joseph was not.

Many people have a dream about what they want to do with their lives. For some, it is simply a fantasy about a way of life that is different from their own. They long for it but do nothing about it. For others, however, this dream becomes a motivating force in their lives. It shapes their education, their work assignments, and the passion is turned into reality. Joseph is one of those and he had a dream about a leadership role he would later have.

In his book *Your Deepest Dream*, Joseph Castleberry shares the story of Randy Borman. He was born in Ecuador of missionary parents and attended Michigan State University. While there, he dreamed of going back to Ecuador and helping the native people. I appreciate the way Castleberry describes what happened in Randy's life:

Randy Borman is what I would call a successful dreamer. Not only has he dreamed, but he has allowed his dream to mature in ways that have inspired him to achieve real depth in his life. Unfortunately, many people are not successful dreamers. Their dreams have either died or never been developed.[2]

It is interesting to note Jacob's reaction to Joseph's dream. The text says, "His brothers were jealous of him, but his father kept the matter in mind" (Genesis 37:11). Maybe Jacob had seen something in Joseph and was able to look past his youthful behavior, weighing it against the integrity he admired in his son.

3

THE FIRST LEADERSHIP ASSIGNMENT

Joseph was about to be given his first leadership assignment—and as we will see, he was not ready for it. His brothers had gone off to Shechem, and Jacob wanted Joseph to check up on them. His instructions were, "Go and see if all is well with your brothers and with the flocks, and bring word back to me" (Genesis 37:14).

What sounds like a simple task carries with it some career questions. Apparently Joseph had earned his father's trust and respect, and so his first real leadership role was carrying out the work of his father. This must have seemed promising. Perhaps he would be the next president of the business?

How did he go about this vaguely defined task? He had no cell phone, no e-mail connection. How do you find your brothers with their flocks grazing a long way off? Joseph headed in the general direction of where he thought they might be. But when they weren't in Shechem as he had anticipated, Genesis 37:15–17 tells us:

> A man found him wandering around in the fields and asked him, "What are you looking for?"
>
> He replied, "I'm looking for my brothers. Can you tell me where they are grazing their flocks?"

"They have moved on from here," the man answered. "I heard them say, 'Let's go to Dotham.' "

These diversions were not five-minute exchanges and the process must have taken a long time, but when he arrived at Dotham he found them there.

Joseph showed a characteristic perseverance in pursuing this task. But he made a huge mistake: he was wearing the "ornate robe" his father had given him as a sign of his favor. What was he thinking? Didn't he consider how his brothers would react to this mark of all that was wrong in the family? It was like wearing a red shirt to a bull fight. Apparently, Joseph was good at carrying out the mechanics of what his father asked him to do, but he completely forgot to think about what he would do when he found his brothers. Not surprisingly, his brothers reacted negatively to his new leadership. "They saw him in the distance, and before he reached them, they plotted to kill him" (Genesis 37:18). At this point in his life, Joseph apparently saw leadership as an opportunity for dominance rather than service.

This reminds me of an experience I had late one evening. My family was away and I was just getting home from work, so I decided to stop into a local fast-food restaurant for something to eat. When I walked through the front door, I thought I recognized the young woman at the counter as a former neighbor, but she didn't acknowledge my glance. As I got up to the counter, though, she began barking orders to the other people behind her: "Clean that counter! Get that order ready!" Then she turned to me and said, "Oh, hi, Mr. Erisman."

It seemed that she had confused her role as night manager and leader with an opportunity to exercise power and authority. She wanted to show me her ability to order others around. I am sure that strategy was not very effective, and I hope she has learned more about leadership since then. Real leadership involves serving others, creating a vision that others will follow.

Jesus told his disciples, "The kings of the Gentiles lord it over them. . . . But you are not to be like that. Instead, the greatest among you should be like the youngest, and the one who rules like the one who serves" (Luke 22:25, 26–27).

Joseph lacked awareness of how his actions and words would affect other people. Scientific research has given us some insight into something called "theory of mind," which John Medina describes in his best-selling book *Brain Rules: 12 Principles for Surviving and Thriving at Work, Home, and School* (Pear Press, 2014). How do people understand a situation from the perspective of others? How does a person get inside the minds of others and imagine what it would be like to experience rewards and punishments from their perspective? This is an incredibly important capability for any leader, and Joseph apparently did not have it yet.

By contrast, Wayne Alderson, vice president of Pittron Steel Company near Pittsburgh in the late 1970s, truly demonstrated "theory of mind." Unlike many executive business leaders in that era (and in the present day), he saw the union—and the people in that union—not as the enemy but as the people who did hard work for the company. He therefore valued them and their work, and he always tried to look at the situation through their eyes.

He walked into a labor management dispute at Pittron as tense and broken as the relationship between Joseph and his brothers. He wanted to break the adversarial relationship that had existed there for so long, but to do so he had to make himself vulnerable and prove he meant what he said. Here, in his own words, is what he did:

> Though I was not on the negotiating team, I entered into a discussion with Sam Piccolo, the union representative, and his men to break the logjam, and the strike was finally settled. The battle in the workplace was fought by men and women who desperately wanted to be treated with value. This was key to settling the strike, and became a key to everything I have done

since. I am not an arbitrator, a mediator, or a negotiator. I am a peacemaker.

My father was a coal miner. He had a thirst and hunger to be treated with dignity and respect. In his life working in the mines, he would come home and say to my mother, "I just want to be seen by management as important as the mule." This concern burned in me, forcing me to see the workers in a different light.

I tried to put in place anything that would demonstrate to people that they were valued. It included things like painting the factory and cleaning the windows so that light could come in. It had been a horrible place to work before, and we wanted to make it attractive. Sam Piccolo, the union president, always did his work from the cab of a crane, but we wanted to demonstrate his value, and the value of the position. So we gave him an office.

I would go down to the gate at shift change to shake hands with the employees and thank them for a good day's work. I learned their names and called them by name. It is a difficult thing to stand at the gate at the end of a shift. You are naked there, but I was motivated to do it because I believed it was right. Some people didn't know what to make of this and would walk by with their heads down. But over time they came to see that the efforts were sincere, that change was real, and they began to raise their heads and talk. I empowered my managers and walked them through this new way of leading. Together we started Operation Turnaround and set the course for a new way to manage. I was not pro-management or pro-union. I was pro-people. The principles are rooted in treating individuals with love, dignity, and respect.

We also committed to improving communications. People needed to know how we were doing, and this meant being very open and honest about everything. Sam Piccolo embraced the vision and joined with me to fight for the "new" style of management [which we called "Value of the Person"]. It was win-win for everyone. I gave special attention to frontline supervisors, one of the most ripped-off groups in management. While the union kicks them in the backside, management is quick to blame them for all the mistakes, while taking credit when things go well. So these frontline supervisors needed to experience love, dignity, and respect. As they experienced a change, they began to change themselves and lead the charge for the Value of the Person. These are just a few examples of changes that led to our success.

The results were unbelievable: a united work force and an outstanding bottom line. To this day, I have a hard time understanding the scope of what happened. But I know this: the change was real because we reached the people. As I conduct seminars and consult with companies today, I find that those who embrace these same principles and implement the leadership of the Value of the Person experience the same dramatic results as we did at Pittron.[1]

In seeing the situation through the eyes of those he was leading, Wayne was able to provide true servant leadership. He was effective in motivating people because he cared about them and understood their perspective. He did not approach them from a position of power.

Perhaps Joseph was naive. We could say that he was naive for telling his brothers and his father his dreams. He was naive for wearing the special coat his father had for him. He was naive for not understanding how his brothers regarded him as he approached them. Or was he arrogant? Did he know how his brothers felt, but did these things nonetheless just because he could? Or was he just not ready for such a leadership assignment?

Again, to cut Joseph a bit of slack, I well remember my first leadership assignment at Boeing. I was selected to lead a ten-person research team although I was one of its youngest members. At first, I was more concerned with what they thought about me than what I could do for them. Leadership requires a level of maturity I didn't have at the time, and it took a while to change my own perspective. Reading R. C. Sproul's book on Wayne Alderson's life a few years later was a helpful step for me. Joseph didn't have such a resource. In any case, he was unprepared for what he would encounter next with his brothers.

4

A ROUGH START

In real life, the start of a bad day looks no different from the start of a good day. There is no ominous music preparing us for what is to come. No tell-tale signs. Then, suddenly, the whole world changes.

The day had started full of promise for Joseph. He was trusted by his father, deputized to provide leadership for the business, responsible for those older and more experienced than he, and asked to report back, almost as the associate director of the family business—and all of this at age seventeen. No doubt Joseph had every reason to be optimistic, so he would have been completely unprepared for what was to follow.

As the brothers saw Joseph coming from a long way off, they recognized him immediately because of his coat. In their rage, they planned to kill him. But the oldest brother Reuben stood up for him, suggesting they detain him and not shed his blood. He had in mind that he could rescue him later and get him back to their father. So the brothers agreed to strip Joseph of his multicolored coat and put him in a cistern alive.

But while Reuben was away, the other brothers conceived another plan. They saw a caravan of Ishmaelites coming from Gilead on their way to Egypt with their camels loaded with spices, an early picture of global trade. By selling Joseph as a slave to the caravan, they could avoid killing him and gain some money at the same time. So they made the sale. Then they killed a goat, put its blood on the coat, and returned the coat to their father, describing the terrible fate that must have befallen Joseph. Naturally, Jacob was devastated. Not only had he lost his son, he had also lost the one he favored and the one perhaps best suited to carry on the family work. I wonder if Jacob realized that he had set Joseph up for this fall by sending him out as he had.

When the caravan arrived in Egypt, Joseph was sold as a slave to the house of Potiphar, the captain of the guard for the Pharaoh. It would have been easy for Joseph to be self-critical at this point. *Why did I wear that coat? Why did I go to my brothers so arrogantly?* Or to blame others. *Why did my father send me into that mess? Why are my brothers so horrible? Where is this God I have worshipped? I have followed him more faithfully than my brothers or even my father, and yet he doesn't seem to care about me.* Or simply to sulk. *Why am I in this terrible mess? I don't deserve this.*

But it appears that Joseph did none of these things. The Bible says he remained connected with his God even in a place far away from home, and he applied himself to the work put in front of him. "The LORD was with Joseph so that he prospered, and he lived in the house of his Egyptian master" (Genesis 39:2).

Joseph ignored his failure and immediately got to work on the next opportunity, in this case in Potiphar's house. And he did this work so well that he got promoted again:

> Joseph found favor in [his master's] eyes, and became his attendant. Potiphar put him in charge of his household, and he entrusted to his care everything he owned. . . . The blessing of the LORD was on everything Potiphar had, both in the house and in the field. So Potiphar left in Joseph's care everything he had; with Joseph in charge, he did not concern himself with anything except the food he ate. (Genesis 39:4–6)

Joseph found himself in a new leadership position—although as a slave, it was not one he would have chosen. He was certainly a long way from home and its familiar surroundings, but he knew his assignment and did it well. He seems to have seen everything he did as God's assignment for his life.

Recovery from failure, even when we contribute to that failure, is an important attribute for all of us. It is too easy to lapse into a "pity party" bemoaning our fate. Interestingly, this ability to start over the way Joseph did is a key to modern-day business as well and is at the heart of the success of Silicon Valley companies that are known as leaders of the tech business.

In an interview for *Ethix,* I talked with Guy Kawasaki, a tech leader in Silicon Valley, about failure and recovery. He had had a very successful career as an Apple "evangelist," working with software teams to develop software for the fledgling Apple Computer Company. Now an author and venture capitalist, he works with entrepreneurs in tech startups in Silicon Valley.

When I asked him what it was about Silicon Valley that created such a great environment for starting a company, he replied,

> In Silicon Valley people are expected to start companies. If you work for a company for 20 years, a lot of people will wonder why you never started a company. In most of the world, if you quit a job after 20 years, people wonder what went wrong. Second, failing isn't that big a deal in Silicon Valley. The odds are bad that any startup is going to succeed. In other parts of the world if you fail, you bring shame and damnation to your family for the next five generations.[1]

Joseph might have been in Silicon Valley—except in his case, he was not starting his own company, but working as a slave. In this position, he did what he was told. Here, he provides a model for every worker in a similar position. His work was not of his choosing, not using all of his leadership skills, and not in a place where he wanted to be. Yet he worked hard, gained trust, and honored God in the position he had at the time.

Before he could get too comfortable even in this position of leading the household of Potiphar, there was more trouble ahead—and this time it was not of his own making.

5

SEXUAL TEMPTATION

Joseph was doing his work in Potiphar's house when he was approached by his master's wife. She wasn't subtle; she saw his attractiveness and propositioned him directly: "Come to bed with me!" (Genesis 39:7). Joseph was in his late teens, with all of the associated hormones. Potiphar's wife was attractive. She was also in a position of authority over him that could make or break his career, such as it was for a head slave in Egypt. The fact that he was far away from home could also have entered his mind in another way. Who would know? He knew no one in that land. With all of these factors, it would have been easy for Joseph to make a short-term decision. He could have avoided carefully thinking through reasons why he should resist, or the consequences of giving in.

Too often we react in the moment. Long term, it is apparent that Joseph was in a no-win situation. Giving in would surely have led to serious consequences for him, but saying no had consequences as well, as we shall see. But he said no and offered two reasons. His first was his commitment to his master, her husband: "My master has withheld nothing from me except you, because you are his wife. How then could I do such a wicked thing?" (Genesis 39:9). And his second reason was that it would be a "sin against God" (Genesis 39:9). In spite of being far from home and any others who shared his faith, Joseph had kept his connection with his God. At least as interesting is what he didn't say: "What if we get caught?" Understanding the consequences of one's behavior is an important thing. But Joseph was even more concerned with what was intrinsically right or wrong about the situation.

Potiphar's wife didn't give up after this direct and straightforward rejection. One day when he went to the house to do his work and there was no one else around, "she caught him by his cloak and said, 'Come to bed with me!' But he left his cloak in her hand and ran out of the house" (Genesis 39:12). In modern language, what Potiphar's wife did was not just inappropriate sexual conduct in the workplace but an abuse of power. It was sexual harassment based on power and position.

Joseph's action reminds me of one of the Proverbs (4:14–15), which to this day I can hear my mother saying,

> Do not set foot on the path of the wicked
>   or walk in the way of evil men.
> Avoid it, do not travel on it;
>   turn from it and go on your way.

Whether or not Joseph thought Potiphar's wife would back off as she had before when he rejected her advances, he was unprepared for the turn of events that followed.

> She called her household servants. "Look," she said to them, "this Hebrew has been brought to us to make sport of us. He came in here to sleep with me. When he heard me scream for help he left his cloak beside me and ran out of the house." . . . When his master heard the story his wife told him . . . he burned with anger. Joseph's master took him and put him in prison, the place where the king's prisoners were confined. (Genesis 39:14–15, 19–20)

Joseph acted more honorably than President Clinton, Pastor Jimmy Swaggart, King David, or a host of other leaders who have fallen to sexual temptation. Further, all of these were the ones in the position of power, not the subordinates. These examples demonstrate the power of sexual attraction, as each person risked dishonoring God and public reputation but gave in anyway.

How was Joseph able to resist this attraction? Some have suggested that Joseph had an advantage: he did not have to deal with the sex-oriented culture we have today, with images from TV, magazines, and advertising bombarding us with sexual reminders. It was a different time, and perhaps people were simply not as sex-crazed as they are today.

But all you need to do to understand the sexual climate of the culture of Joseph's day is look at the previous chapter, Genesis 38. There we see more than enough sexual perversion to fill any modern-day soap opera, centered on some of the exploits of Joseph's brother Judah and his family. When I was growing up and we would read through the Bible after dinner, I remember my father skipping the thirty-eighth chapter because of its crudeness. Of course, this caused my brothers and me to read it on our own, and I always wondered why it was there in the middle of the story of Joseph. But now it seems to me that it is here to establish the climate in which Joseph made his choice.

Sexually inappropriate behavior, one of the trifecta of temptations (money, sex, and power), is unfortunately too common in business situations and creates painful devastation for the individuals and sometimes the company involved. We often associate sexual temptation with the West, where sexuality is embedded in so much of the media and entertainment. But this is a worldwide challenge. For example, Malaysian Methodist bishop Hwa Yung reminds us:

> The external pressures faced by Christians in the marketplace in Asia are the same as those faced by Christians worldwide. They can be summed up by the words "money, sex, and power". Christians often fail to take seriously the corrupting power of these three forces.[1]

Of course, this is not just a challenge for Christians, or even religious people. Anyone can be hurt by the consequences of yielding to such temptation. Both Harry Stonecipher (former CEO of

Boeing) and Mark Hurd (former CEO of Hewlett-Packard) lost jobs and reputations, and in Stonecipher's case a fifty-year marriage, because of this type of scandal.

Sexually inappropriate behavior is often associated with predatory men, but that was not the case for Joseph. In the 1994 movie *Disclosure,* the inventor and founder of a technology company, played by Michael Douglas, is sexually attacked by the company president, played by Demi Moore. It is, however, Michael Douglas's character who is accused and threatened. Audiences were surprised to see a woman portrayed as the one doing the harassment. Stories like Joseph's should remind us, though, that none of us is immune from temptation. No matter who we are, we need to be prepared to resist the enticements of money, sex, and power.

Although Scripture doesn't tell us much about *how* Joseph resisted temptation, we can see some patterns. Tim Keller writes in *Counterfeit Gods: The Empty Promises of Money, Sex, and Power, and the Only Hope that Matters*, "Idolatry is not just a failure to obey God; it is a setting of the whole heart on something besides God."[2] Joseph couldn't set his whole heart on an idol when his heart was set on God. He recognized, and verbalized, that giving in would have meant abandoning God: "How could I do such a wicked thing and sin against God?" This kind of resistance against temptation can come only from preparation. His confident response shows that Potiphar's wife did not catch him off guard.

A modern-day leader, General Peter Pace, former chair of the Joint Chiefs of Staff, told me how he prepared for the temptations of his office:

> I went to National Security Council meetings three times a week with the president of the United States. I knew what the topic was going to be. I would think through while I was shaving that morning the things I would allow myself to say yes to, and things I knew I would say no to, and the things I needed to make sure

I got across in that meeting. I was not always right, but I always spoke my mind. My truth was a piece of the whole truth that everybody needed to look at, along with the other viewpoints in the room. But at least I knew going in, generically, who I wanted to be coming out. I told myself if I heard anything in there that I was not comfortable with, I was going to speak up, and for sure I was going to say these things. That strategy enabled me to be forearmed for the unexpected things that would inevitably come up in such a meeting.[3]

While General Pace was dealing with a large set of temptation issues, his advice applies well to the case of sexual temptation. Anticipate the situations where you might find yourself and prepare for how you would respond.

There are plenty of opportunities for today's businesspeople, both men and women, to get caught away from home, perhaps on a business trip, or working closely with another person for long hours on a job. Where it is easy to get caught up with the crowd, group dynamics can take over. Keeping a close connection with God and preparing in advance for what might happen are two important strategies for resistance. Joseph offers us a model for staying centered in God and being prepared for dealing with sexual temptation.

6

WHEN BAD THINGS HAPPEN TO GOOD PEOPLE

Sometimes in the midst of difficult circumstances we can see God teaching us something we need to learn. More often, however, we see how an event shaped our lives only much later, as in the case of Joseph. He found himself the victim of Potiphar's wife's unwanted advances, and when he tried to do the right thing, he was convicted on false charges. Joseph was now not only a slave in a foreign land but also in prison. It must have seemed like a very bad day at the end of a very bad year for Joseph.

Some argue that if you do the right thing, it will pay off for you in the end. But when Joseph rejected Potiphar's wife's advances, he did the right thing simply because it was right, not because of how it might work out. If making a difficult choice to do the right thing always brought good results, then ethics would simply be a part of everyone's business strategy. It is not. We are often called on to make the right choice when we don't know how or even if it can work out. For Joseph, the wrong he suffered as a result of his choice was eventually made right, but he was thirty years old before that resolution came. For some, it never works out.

Business ethics (making right choices in a business situation) is a challenge for leaders at every level and in all parts of the world. I was once speaking to an audience in Beijing on the subject of why we should act ethically in business. My argument included all of the usual reasons for why acting ethically is generally best for business, but I closed with two important personal reasons: You will need to look yourself in the mirror the next morning and live with the choices you have made. Ultimately, you should choose to do the right thing because it is right, not because of the results. One young man raised his hand and asked, "I am starting a small business. It is tough to get started with many obstacles. Wouldn't it be okay for me to put off looking at ethics until I have established my business? Do I need to consider ethics now?" I responded with the following:

> Here are some questions for you to think about in answering that question. What do you mean by *established*? If you don't set that point now, you will never set it. There will always be a reason to say it is not yet time to start acting ethically. Second, who will retrain you and all of your employees to begin to follow ethical practices once you have reached your objective? You will suddenly need to start acting differently, and you may have hired all of the wrong people. Third, do you enjoy doing business with people who act unethically? Do you feel comfortable making agreements with someone who is out to cheat you? Finally, how would you feel about building a company that you were not proud of?

He smiled and simply said, "You win," and then sat down. I reminded him that while this was no guarantee for success, it was an important step in the right direction in any case.

Bookstores are filled with titles arguing that good choices are rewarded, that good ethics is good business, live right and you will live well. In the long run, and with the right measures of success, this is true. But we must be honest. Living right can also have negative consequences. It is important to make right choices, but we shouldn't be deluded into thinking that these right choices will always pay off for us, particularly in the short run. And the word *short* is open to interpretation.

We need to be prepared to make the right choices and know that they have consequences. Sometimes bad things happen to good people. How do we choose between right and wrong in a difficult situation beyond our control, when there is no clear way to see how any good can come from it?

Steve Bell, a cabinet maker and small business owner, had a day early in his own career when he, like Joseph, made good choices but wound up in a difficult place. Here is his story:

> I launched my business with a little company called Bell Specialty Woodcraft in the late 1970s. I was basically a handyman-type guy who would do anything that was honest and legal having to do with carpentry. I started remodeling houses, and then I built a couple of new houses. I was introduced to a dentist by my plumber and started remodeling this dentist's home. He seemed to have a lot of money and was spending it. He introduced me to one of his friends who owned a dental supply company in Seattle and in a very short period of time, I was into the dental office business, building new dental offices and remodeling old ones. We incorporated as Belcon Construction and Development Corporation in September of 1980. By 1981, I had seven or eight employees, and we were doing dental-office work from Everett to south of Olympia in the state of Washington, over about a seventy-mile span.
>
> I thought I was God's gift to the world of business. Here everybody was in recession (remember at this time interest rates were about 20 percent) and I was just booming, making the best money I had ever made in my life.
>
> Then in the spring of 1981, I got a phone call from my attorney one morning and he said, "Steve, are you sitting down? Your dentist buddy is on the front page of the paper. He was just arrested in a sting operation with a briefcase full of cocaine. All of his assets have been seized." My whole world came crashing down around our business and our family. My wife, Carolyn, and I were left holding the bag for over $100,000 worth of bills associated with the dental clinics under construction, and at that time that was a substantial amount of money. We had two small children, and the third child was on the way. We had no medical insurance and a ton of medical bills. Life became very desperate.[1]

Both Steve Bell and Joseph were trapped in difficult circumstances by forces outside of their control. They had made honest and right choices, but that wasn't enough. You can feel the devastation each one faced. Fortunately, this was not the end of the story for Steve Bell or for Joseph.

7

COMMITMENT
TO THE TASK

What do you do when, through no fault of your own, you find yourself in a desperate situation? If it is sympathy you want, there may be plenty of people to commiserate with, but then what?

In the last chapter, we left Joseph falsely accused and in prison in a foreign land. He must have felt utterly alone. We left Steve Bell with a young family, no work, and a pile of unpaid bills. What did they do in these situations, and what can we learn from them? Both Joseph and Steve Bell had an important support for their position. Both had confidence in God. We will pick up with Joseph's story first.

> But while Joseph was there in prison, the LORD was with him; he showed him kindness and granted him favor in the eyes of the prison warden. So the warden put Joseph in charge of all those held in the prison, and he was made responsible for all that was done there. The warden paid no attention to anything under Joseph's care, because the LORD was with Joseph and gave him success in whatever he did. (Genesis 39:20–23)

Once again, Joseph's character and commitment to God shine through. He was back in a leadership position again, even second in command again. But remember his career trajectory. He was second in command for his father's business. Then second in command among the slaves in Potiphar's house. Now he was second in command among the prisoners in a jail. This is not exactly a career path most people would choose.

But for Joseph the key focus was to get back to work, using his gifts and abilities and working hard regardless of the circumstances. As we saw when Joseph was in Potiphar's house, the vital step was for him was to do what he had been given to do with all of his heart. His dependence on God seemed to be at the center of his focus on his work.

Of course, it can be especially difficult to feel motivated to do one's best at work after such a crushing disappointment as Joseph had experienced. From an outside perspective, Joseph's work in prison might have seemed pointless: no matter how well he managed his fellow prisoners, he was unlikely to be released. What must his attitude have been like to achieve success in the face of such discouraging circumstances?

Most of us can probably relate to Joseph, because we have also been in difficult situations. One of the leaders I interviewed for *Ethix* had particular insight into how Joseph may have handled this disappointing development. Tami Heim has been a senior executive in retailing for many years, including as the president of Borders until she left in 2005 (the company's last profitable year). Her career has also had ups and downs, and I asked her what advice she would offer someone who was not in an ideal position. She said,

> It's easy to get sidetracked thinking about everything else instead of what's the real priority. If a manager can stay focused on the assignment at hand and not be preoccupied with what's the next position, doors and opportunities will open. I always encourage managers to do their best right where they are. I have seen that truth at work in my own life. Don't spend time creating reasons or excuses for why you're not able to do something. If you do, then you're missing out on how you can empower yourself. Adopt the mind-set that says, "What do I need to do differently to achieve a different outcome?" You can't change others but you

can always change yourself. It's all about attitude. Only you can choose your attitude every day, and it makes a difference if you choose it wisely.[1]

Let's see how Steve Bell handled his difficult situation. When we left him, he had developed his cabinet-making business with a focus on dental clinics, with most of the work for one client. When the client was arrested for money laundering and drug smuggling, he was left with $100,000 in bills, a growing family, and seemingly nowhere to go. Again, in his words from our 2007 interview:

> When I look back on that situation, I realize my role in this was very significant. I was naive, very inexperienced, and had no business training. I was headstrong and arrogant. These guys took advantage of me, but I should have seen it coming.
>
> My client had been involved in drug smuggling and money laundering schemes, and the IRS and the drug enforcement agency seized all of the assets. I remember sitting down at a conference table with my attorney and accountant, and they said, "Steve, you have just been had. We don't see any option for you except to file bankruptcy."
>
> All I could think about was my dad, who had taught me to be a man of my word. "Your word is your bond," he told me. "The only thing you could carry through your whole life is your name."
>
> So I told my attorney I had made a commitment, and I couldn't take the easy way out. He responded, "Son, son, you just don't understand. Within months you will have a dozen lawsuits filed against you. You have to file for protection." But I said, "Perhaps I do, but first I am going to try it my way."
>
> I wrote a letter to every single person I owed money to, and then followed up with a personal visit or a phone call and just asked them to trust me.
>
> We spent the next six years of our lives paying off these bills. We never asked for a dime of discount and paid every debt with interest. The only thing I asked from people I owed money to was to trust me and let me pay them on my terms and not theirs. So, every month for six years, every single person I owed money

to heard from us either in the form of a check or a phone call. I owed Continental Hardwoods $5,000, and I can remember writing them a check for $5 one month because that was all I could afford. But every month they got something from me, and I paid that debt off in about five years. Today I do a substantial business with them on an unsecured open line of credit.

Not one person ever sued us. If they had, it would have forced us into bankruptcy. Some of them were irritated, some of them were hurt, but once they realized that I was chipping away at it, they stuck with us. Today, I have some great fans in this local industry right now who were partners during that time. There isn't one of them who would not do business with us today.[2]

We can see some strong commonalities in these stories. First, Steve identified his own role in what happened. We don't know if Joseph ever saw how his actions with his brothers had contributed to his problems. Second, and very much like Joseph, Steve worked in a creative way. Rather than sulking, both Steve and Joseph got to work in the situation where they found themselves. Third, doing the right thing did not make things better instantly. It was a long haul for both of them.

There is an important footnote to Steve's story. In a fairytale, once everything is resolved, they live "happily ever after." Not so in the real world of business. Steve's business had grown dramatically, and in 2005 he was recognized as Small Businessperson of the Year in the state of Washington, which even gave him a chance to meet with the president of the United States. He had numerous honors from industry associations. His factory was a model of modern business practices, with lean manufacturing (even The Boeing Company came to see what he was doing) and sustainability practices that captured every stray drop of varnish in the production process of making cabinets.

But then, at the end of 2008, the economic crisis hit. All building stopped, and there was little market for his products. Being in the middle of such a situation is not as easy as looking back on it after things have improved. During that time I asked Steve how it was going, to which he responded: "We need to be reminded every once in a while who's really in control. God is faithful. Through it all we grow and get stronger."

8

A GLIMMER OF HOPE

In a difficult and dark period, we look for a light at the end of the tunnel. And we hope it is not the headlight of an oncoming train!

Joseph had been in slavery and in prison for eleven years, with no evidence that his situation would change. But then an opportunity came his way that opened a small ray of hope. He was joined in the prison by two of Pharaoh's key officials: his chief cupbearer and his chief baker. We don't know what they had done that led to their imprisonment, but as we saw earlier, justice was not the norm in Egypt at that time. Pharaoh's anger with them was apparently enough. Since Joseph was responsible for the prisoners, naturally the two came under his care.

One morning Joseph saw that the two officials of Pharaoh looked dejected, and he initiated a conversation with them. Seeing the situation of another through their eyes was something Joseph was not able to do earlier, but it seems this was a skill he had gained in prison. He learned that they had each had a dream the night before and were concerned because there was no one to tell them what their dreams meant.

Earlier, Joseph had a dream that gave him a vision of a future that no longer seemed possible at this point. His father and brothers were a long way away and only a distant memory. They were not about to bow down to him anytime soon! But apparently

Joseph still believed in God and trusted God. And he believed that God could give insight into the meaning of dreams. He seems to have been undeterred by the outcome of his own dream, because he told the men that with God's help he would listen to their dreams and share whatever insight God might provide.

The chief cupbearer went first. He told of a dream involving three branches in front of him that blossomed and produced grapes. He picked the grapes, squeezed them into Pharaoh's cup, and gave the cup to Pharaoh. Joseph told the chief cupbearer that his dream indeed had a meaning. The three branches were three days. In three days, he would be back in Pharaoh's palace resuming his duties as the chief cupbearer.

But then Joseph made a request. He explained to the chief cupbearer that he was in prison under false charges. He had been sold into slavery from the land of the Hebrews, falsely accused and in prison though he had done nothing wrong. "When all goes well with you," he said, "remember me and show me kindness; mention me to Pharaoh and get me out of this prison" (Genesis 40:14).

Perhaps heartened by the good news for the chief cupbearer, the chief baker also told his dream to Joseph. In his dream there were three baskets of bread on his head, but the birds were eating the bread from the baskets. Unfortunately, Joseph had bad news for the chief baker. He told him that in three days he would be executed.

In three days, it was Pharaoh's birthday, and on that day Pharaoh gave a large feast. Just as Joseph had said, the chief cupbearer was restored to his position by Pharaoh, but the chief baker was put to death.

We can learn important things about leadership and attitude from this part of the story. Joseph did not lose his connection with God, even after this extended time in prison. In fact, his interaction with God seemed as fresh and natural as it was earlier. He recognized that God, not he, was the one who could interpret dreams, and he trusted and had confidence in his God. So he gave credit to God for his insight in a deliberate way. It is too easy to call on God when we are in trouble and claim credit for ourselves when we have a great insight. The deliberate act of crediting God also served as a check on Joseph's ego. This serves as a good model for each of us.

We also see he was straightforward in his communication. He had bad news to deliver, and he did so compassionately but honestly. Delivering bad news is difficult, whether it is to a subordinate or to a superior. Joseph would need to deliver bad news to a superior later, and this might seem even more difficult, but delivering it to a subordinate is also tough. It was a fundamental part of leadership then and remains fundamental now.

Jack Welch, the iconic CEO and chairman of General Electric, talked about the importance of being honest and clear in communication in a 2001 lecture he gave at Fairfield University.[1] He advised that while sugar-coating bad news, particularly in a performance review with a subordinate, may seem kind, in the end it is very unkind. He told of a person at GE who had been with the company for twenty years when his job was terminated. This person had been in the wrong place, unable to perform well, for many years. But year after year, his supervisors had been unwilling to deliver bad news and instead told him that his performance was great. Now in his forties, he had never had the opportunity to find a position to which he was better suited. He drifted for so long that it would be more difficult now for him to find the right spot. None of his supervisors did him a favor by allowing him to get by, Welch said. It would have been more compassionate to tell it straight and help the person get the training and tools to be effective.

Another form of this problem occurs when a leader wants to avoid responsibility for a decision. I remember the time I was talking with a person in my organization who asked me why I didn't approve a pay increase for him. After investigating what had happened, I found that his manager had been unwilling to make the hard choices about how to allocate the money she had available for her organization. She simply told everyone they deserved a large raise, but of course, I had vetoed it. Clearly, this was a problem I needed to sort out with her!

The third thing we see from Joseph is his attitude about where he was. As I said before, he didn't sulk; he did what was assigned, and he did it well. But he was not content to remain in that position. His message to the chief cupbearer was simply a reminder to act kindly toward him and remember him to Pharaoh. I have encountered too many followers of God who assume God is in control and therefore there is nothing for them to do. Joseph found the balance of trust and initiative and seemed to handle it well.

In the preface, I described my own "prison" experience at work. I don't believe I did as well as Joseph at recognizing that I could trust God with the circumstances and realize that he was with me in them. In retrospect, I whined a bit too much. But ultimately I did come around to getting back to work in spite of the circumstances.

Finally, the fact that he had been in prison eleven years already tells us that situations don't necessarily get better instantly! Sometimes we believe that if we trust God and do the right thing, everything will immediately fall in place. Not so. In a broken world, things don't always work out as they should. All of us are forced to work through some pain, disappointment, and misunderstanding. Joseph offers us a model for how to do this.

I can imagine Joseph saw a glimmer of hope in this moment. For the first time he was able to make his case to a person who had the ear of Pharaoh. And though justice was not assured, at least there was a possibility that his case would be heard.

Unfortunately, "The chief cupbearer . . . did not remember Joseph; he forgot him" (Genesis 40:23).

9

THE OPPORTUNITY AT THE RIGHT TIME

Just as there is no ominous music, gathering of clouds, or any other sign to announce bad events in our lives (except in the movies), so a good day begins as any other. Joseph was going about his day as he had for almost five thousand previous days in prison. It had been two years since the chief cupbearer returned to his position, forgetting about Joseph. Perhaps Joseph had settled back into the pattern of work he'd kept before he saw that opportunity. Like many people today, he may have assumed that this was his long-term assignment, and so he refocused his work in this direction. In spite of the opportunity that soon was going to change his course, we should not lose sight of the lessons we can learn from Joseph's example of working hard and well in difficult circumstances.

But there was a commotion going on in the palace of Pharaoh. Pharaoh had had a dream, actually two dreams, and none of the wise men on his staff were able to tell him what these dreams meant. Had the chief cupbearer not remembered what had happened two years earlier, Joseph would likely have had some new prisoners to take care of. But the chief cupbearer finally remembered the message he was supposed to have passed on and said to Pharaoh,

> Today I am reminded of my shortcomings. Pharaoh was once angry with his servants, and he imprisoned me and the chief

baker in the house of the captain of the guard. Each of us had a dream the same night, and each dream had a meaning of its own. Now a young Hebrew was there with us, a servant of the captain of the guard. We told him our dreams, and he interpreted them for us, giving each man the interpretation of his dream. And things turned out exactly as he interpreted them to us: I was restored to my position, and the other man was impaled. (Genesis 41:9–13)

So Pharaoh sent for Joseph.

Put yourself in Joseph's position for a moment. After all this time, he had the opportunity for release. He was bypassing the bureaucracy, going right to the top! These situations come up often in the workplace. People in business are familiar with the tendency to treat another person as an opportunity for advancing their own cause. A salesperson meets another parent at his child's school and wonders if this new acquaintance might represent an opportunity for a sale. An employee is concerned about his or her position in the organization and gets an opportunity to meet with the president. A person is out of work and connects with a senior executive at a company where he would like to be employed.

As Joseph was called to this meeting with Pharaoh, he faced three questions: How should he prepare for the meeting? How should he speak to such a powerful leader? Should he use his knowledge as a bargaining tool to get out of prison? We will deal with these questions in subsequent chapters, but for now let's consider the question of the timing of this event.

Joseph's opportunity to stand before Pharaoh came about because the chief cupbearer had forgotten the prisoner's request until just this moment. What would have happened if the chief cupbearer had brought the information to Pharaoh two years earlier? It seems unlikely that Joseph would have had the same opportunity. The cupbearer, having just been released from prison, would likely have been on tenuous ground with Pharaoh. Would Pharaoh have listened to him? Would he have done anything for Joseph? Two years earlier, Pharaoh had not needed someone to interpret his dreams, but now he did. The opportunity for Joseph came because of Pharaoh's need, not because of Joseph's plight. So in business today, timing—which is often out of our control—is critical.

Bill Gates comments on the importance of timing in his own career in his book *The Road Ahead.*

> My friend Warren Buffett, who's often called the world's greatest investor, talks about how grateful he is to live at a time when his particular talents are valuable. Warren says if he'd been born a few thousand years ago, he'd probably have been some animal's lunch. But he was born into an age that has a stock market and rewards Warren for his unique understanding of the market.
>
> Football stars should feel grateful too, Warren says. "There just happens to be a game, where it turns out that a guy who can kick a ball with a funny shape through goal posts a fair percentage of the time can make millions of dollars a year."[1]

Then Gates goes on to talk about his own upbringing on the Eastside of Seattle, with supportive parents and his education at a private school where he met Paul Allen, at a time when the computing industry was just coming alive. Together they formed Microsoft and the rest is history.

In my position at Boeing, I certainly had my share of moments when I saw the importance of timing in the success of our work. In the early 1990s, one of the top researchers on my Boeing R&D staff developed some mathematical strategies for managing the complexity of the airplane assembly line. The goal was to assure that all of the parts needed at any stage of the assembly would be available at the time they were needed, thus assuring a smooth flow of production. We made a presentation to a gathering of executives and technical leaders in the two different assembly divisions of the airplane company, expecting they would be excited about the new capability we laid out.

Instead, the presentation was halted by a rather heated discussion between key analysts from the two divisions as to which side had the best present capability. No one was listening to our great breakthrough. As the meeting broke up, one of the vice presidents came up to me, put his arm on my shoulder, and said, "Al, I don't think we are ready for this solution." We were very disappointed.

Five years later, I received a call in my office from the vice president of one of the assembly areas. They were trying to ramp up production, and everything was getting bogged down by parts shortages. It would cost millions to shut down the assembly line, but he remembered that we might have something to help them. Now the time was right, and the new mathematical strategy made a huge difference for the company. It hadn't worked before, not because of our solution itself, but because the timing wasn't right.

We live in an era when patience is often not valued. The old prayer "Lord, give me patience and I want it right now" reminds us of our demand for an instant response. Technology and instant messaging only heighten that expectation. A colleague and I have done research on which of the fruits of the Spirit is most valued in business today, and we found that few organizations value patience or self-control.[2]

The value of timing, combined with patience, is demonstrated in this crucial part of Joseph's story and offers an important lesson to us in the twenty-first century. God granted favor to Joseph by allowing him to meet with Pharaoh at just the right time.

10

PROFESSIONALISM

There is a little part of this story that is easily overlooked: "So Pharaoh sent for Joseph, and he was quickly brought from the dungeon. When he had shaved and changed his clothes he came before Pharaoh" (Genesis 41:14).

After all this time in prison, it might seem that going unshaven and dirty before Pharaoh would help Joseph establish his case. Joseph had been falsely accused and stuck in prison, and looking the part would help communicate his real situation to Pharaoh. Ultimately, however, Joseph seemed to grasp that this meeting was not about him. He was being called on to solve a problem for Pharaoh. He may have been directed to dress up before going to Pharaoh, we don't know. But as we go on with the story we will see he prepared for the meeting in other ways that showed his professionalism. This kind of respect through dress, language, and preparation that Joseph demonstrates is an area of great importance for business today.

Today's twenty-something young people, the so-called Millennials, are often referred to as the "me" generation. They are known for being forward, brash, focused on themselves, and for living with a sense of entitlement. Of course, such labels are too broad. Not everyone in that age group behaves this way, while many outside the age group do. A business owner said that one of our interns arrived dressed so casually it was embarrassing. Further, the intern would walk into the room and immediately begin making a request. No "excuse me," no "good morning," just interrupting the boss in the middle of another conversation. This owner said the intern was a good worker and smart, but needed a great deal of coaching about appropriate workplace behavior. At the School of Business, Government, and Economics at Seattle Pacific University where I teach, there are enough indications of these characteristics that we decided to do something.

This led us to begin a focus on professionalism, broadly defined. We started with "Professional Wednesday," when students (and professors!) are expected to dress in business-appropriate attire. It is extended now to role-playing scenarios dealing with communications. It includes a writing expectation for all classes, where part of the grade depends on clear, clean, and well-crafted papers. There may have been a time when students arrived at the university with good writing ability, professional dress, and good manners, but this seems to be less true today. Joseph provides an important model for the importance of these things in a professional setting.

The issue of appropriate dress is not a new issue in business. When I was at Boeing, the technical people on our research staff tended to dress more casually than most at the company. We knew, however, that an executive meeting called for more professional dress, often including ties for men who seldom wore them. Still, one of our best analysts made the mistake once of coming to an executive meeting wearing shorts and flip-flops. As most of the executives were dressed in suits and ties, it was an embarrassing moment. The analyst's casual attire created a problem for the whole research organization when one of the executives took offense.

But the story of Joseph takes us beyond the matter of appropriate dress. As Joseph stood before Pharaoh, here is what Pharaoh said to him:

> "In my [first] dream I was standing on the bank of the Nile, when out of the river there came up seven cows, fat and sleek, and they grazed among the reeds. After them, seven other cows

came up—scrawny and very lean. I had never seen such ugly cows in all the land of Egypt. The lean, ugly cows ate up the seven fat cows that came up first. But even after they ate them, no one could tell that they had done so; they looked just as ugly as before. Then I woke up.

"In my [second] dream I saw seven heads of grain, full and good, growing on a single stalk. After them, seven other heads sprouted—withered and thin and scorched by the east wind. The thin heads of grain swallowed up the seven good heads. I told this to the magicians, but none of them could explain it to me." (Genesis 41:17–24)

We have already seen that Joseph was good at interpreting dreams, but he again took a humble approach here. Joseph had already told Pharaoh that it was God, not he, who could interpret dreams. Then, after listening to Pharaoh's account, Joseph straightforwardly explained the meaning of his dreams: "God has revealed to Pharaoh what he is about to do" (Genesis 41:24). He didn't ask about his own fate. He didn't negotiate for his own position. Instead, he addressed Pharaoh respectfully, directing his energy to solving Pharaoh's problem.

Examining the conversation Joseph had with Pharaoh, it is evident that Joseph was prepared and polite, and that he honored the office of the leader of the country. Joseph's focus was on answering Pharaoh's questions and addressing the problem at hand.

The basic issue here is whether we view people as valuable human beings, treating them with dignity and respect—regardless of their high or low position. The title "Human Resources Department" doesn't help, since it suggests that people are tools to get the job done, not human beings with whom we work.

We have dealt with this issue in KIROS, our organization for Christians in business. People sometimes come to our meetings with their own agendas, seeking a job or business leads, or trying to gain access to business leaders in order to promote their own nonprofit organization. They appear to view others in the room as tools for their own purposes rather than as colleagues.

In one case, a gentleman came to a breakfast meeting wearing a large sign on his back stating that he was looking for a job. Not only was this disruptive, but it also reflected poorly on his own professionalism. Others have come to meetings with a clear goal of selling their services, whether it is life insurance or consulting services. They set up a coffee appointment with someone they meet, but rather than get to know the other person, they immediately launch into their sales pitch. These are fundamental issues of professionalism.

In addressing these concerns, we have put together guidelines for establishing "rooted relationships," built around getting to know the other person and caring about that person first. It is not about what we can get from them, but who they are. Yes, business deals may come out of this relationship, but that should be the byproduct, not the focus. Jack vanHartesvelt, whom we will meet more extensively in chapter 19, often says, "It's not about me, and it's not about right now." This changes our orientation to service.

It is important to notice what Joseph said and didn't say in his conversation with Pharaoh, as well as how he said it. His attitude was one of service, with a focus on addressing the needs of the other person. Yes, Pharaoh held the fate of Joseph in his hands, so it might be assumed that anyone in Joseph's position would act this way out of fear. This is far from true. Almost any recruiting manager could tell stories of the unprofessional way job applicants approach an interview. Fear does not necessarily overcome our desires to put ourselves first. The model of focusing on the needs of others is needed now more than ever. Joseph said nothing about his own circumstances. We will examine another dimension of this conversation in chapter 12, where we deal with how to speak to people in authority.

In chapter 2, we said that Joseph's deep dreams of leadership required maturity. Perhaps his time in prison, where he served with excellence, helped him to finally develop that maturity.

11

OFFICE POLITICS

When Joseph stood before Pharaoh, he faced two potential problems. First, Pharaoh's officials were standing there with him. How much should he say, when he was likely wondering what they might do with the information he was about to share? After that, he still had to reckon with the intimidating power of Pharaoh. How should he speak to such a person? We will deal with the first question in this chapter and the second in the next.

It is commonly said that "knowledge is power" and in this case, Joseph had the knowledge. That power would be gone if he shared all of his insight. A member of Pharaoh's staff might step forward to implement Joseph's plan, and he could be sent back to prison. The behavior of stealing another person's ideas and claiming them as your own is called office politics, and it happens in every office.

But Joseph appears to have ignored this pressure completely, and he simply laid out what he thought Pharaoh needed to know. He told him what the two dreams meant: God had shown Pharaoh the future. There would be seven good years of harvest followed by seven drought years so bad that the good years would be lost in the severity of the famine. The two dreams—the cattle and then the heads of grain—with the same outcome confirmed the urgency of what was certain to occur, and that it was God who had revealed this certainty to him.

Joseph might well have stopped at this point. He had answered Pharaoh's question. But what he said next might be even more surprising in light of the way business is often carried out today. We see no evidence that Joseph was using his knowledge to gain personal advantage. He did not hold back from revealing things to those who might take the information and use their relationship with Pharaoh to advance their own position. Perhaps, unlike business today, no one had an advantage with Pharaoh because he was considered a god above the ordinary people. In any case, Joseph went on:

> "And now let Pharaoh look for a discerning and wise man and put him in charge of the land of Egypt. Let Pharaoh appoint commissioners over the land to take a fifth of the harvest of Egypt during the seven years of abundance. They should collect all the food of these good years that are coming and store up the grain under the authority of Pharaoh, to be kept in the cities for food. This food should be held in reserve for the country, to be used during the seven years of famine that will come upon Egypt, so that the country may not be ruined by the famine." (Genesis 41:33–36)

Joseph simply told it as he saw it, apparently ignoring the potential fallout of what would be done with the news he brought.

I suppose I am sensitive to this issue after long years at Boeing, where like most large organizations (and even small ones) office politics are a way of life. In one instance, I was working for Stan, one of the bosses for whom I had deep admiration at Boeing. He was respectful and encouraging, and I tried to learn from him. He had one practice that I always admired but was never able to emulate. The desk in his office was always clean. And at the end of a meeting he never took an action item, but during that relationship I found myself with multiple special reports to create.

I had been doing a lot of work with our Cray supercomputer for oil companies, and Joel, another person on Stan's staff, was responsible for some work internally with the company. Stan therefore asked us to work together to come up with an approach he could present to some Boeing executives about the potential internal use of our Cray. We were asked to report back to him in his office at 10:00 a.m. on the next Tuesday. After the meeting, Joel came to me and said he had no idea how to approach the problem. He asked to meet me in my office later that morning to sketch out what we would do. Because I was familiar with the question, I was happy to do so, and we sketched out something fairly quickly. I gave Joel some supplemental material and asked him to put his own spin on it, since he knew the internal potential users better than I did. We planned to meet on Monday to review our presentation for Stan.

Monday came and went, and I was unable to reach Joel. On Tuesday, I took what I had put together earlier and went to Stan's office at 9:50 a.m. His door was shut, and there was still no sign of Joel. At about 10:10 a.m. I asked Stan's administrative assistant when our meeting would start and she said she wasn't sure. Then I asked her who was in Stan's office, and she told me that Joel had arrived for a meeting at 9:30. I knocked on the door and went in, and there was Joel sharing the material I had given him with Stan, presenting it as his own. I joined the meeting and we finished going through the material, creating the presentation Stan wanted.

Stan asked me to stay for a few minutes after the meeting and asked me what had been going on. To his credit, he immediately understood, but it was a very disconcerting event.

I used to think there was no such thing as office politics, merely different points of view. But competitive office politics can be devastating. It can stand in the way of getting the best solutions when position and influence replace the free exchange of ideas for achieving the best solution.

I also used to think that office politics were confined to large companies and didn't have a place in smaller companies, educational institutions, or churches. That, too, is not true. I

remember an airplane trip across the country to a mathematics conference with a colleague from the University of British
Columbia. He was chairing a university department and I was
responsible for the mathematics research staff at Boeing. I told
him about my hopes of leaving Boeing at some time to go to a
university—where it was all about the ideas, and where I could
get away from the politics too common in big business. I think
he laughed for ten minutes before he told me how it was. And I
have subsequently come to see that he was right.

It might seem difficult to take Joseph's approach to office
politics when our careers are at stake. Every situation requires
care and insight, but I have found that being straightforward
as much as possible is the best approach. There are people who
are upfront and transparent even in today's competitive business environment. One such person is Pete Fox, former general
manager of sales for Microsoft. In 2010, he told his story to our
KIROS (Christians in business) organization about dealing with
office politics at Microsoft. As you will see, Pete does not advo-
cate a simple, guaranteed-to-win strategy. Rather, he has found
his own way of dealing with a real, competitive environment in a
way that honors his principles. Here is an excerpt from his story:

> I have spent much of my time at Microsoft out in the field of-
> fices. Since my move to headquarters, I've found there are acres
> of people with some of the strangest behaviors I've ever seen. In
> the field sales organization, we had a saying that we have only
> as much political clout as our recent results would allow. If you
> execute well, you have lots of power. Those who don't, have little.
>
> I've also decided to play as little politics as possible, doing
> only what's necessary to keep out of harm's way. What I've
> learned, sadly, is that my strategy of "playing not to lose" repre-
> sents flawed thinking. In politics, there are two choices, "playing
> to win" or "playing to lose." Political animals only see winners
> and losers, and they make up the rules of the game.
>
> I've also seen otherwise committed colleagues turn on one
> another over a budget dollar or incremental headcount alloca-

tion. This behavior seems to be understood and taken in stride by many, when it completely astonishes me.

My thinking is that my word and deeds are all I have for people to judge me by. Especially as a Christian, I know that how I live, the legacy I leave, how I teach and lead others, these are the ways I will be judged one day. That day could be today. I won't wait to leave my legacy and live for God's glory. I do it now, every day and every way I can.

I believe that I am doing God's will by working hard, making Microsoft successful through the software our customers use and derive benefit from. We enable people and businesses to "reach their full potential"—corny as it sounds. So, I have committed to play the role of Boy Scout. This may indeed cause me to be more predictable, politically, than some of my peers. Being more predictable may then make me an easier opponent in the war of perceptions, but it is a choice I have made.

One practical way I work this out might be seen in this example. When I believe it would be beneficial for the business if I took on a part of the organization now reporting to a colleague, I don't start by going to the boss about it. I start by talking with my colleague. I tell him why I believe what I do, and that I will be taking my proposal to the boss. But I don't blindside him with this information.

I'm not standing still and settling for playing not to lose. I have learned how to play to win and keep my relationships whole. But it's not easy.[1]

Joseph and Pete Fox seemed to have followed a similar path. Do what you can to rise above the fray. Take the high road. And recognize that there is no guarantee that this will bring the best result for you.

12

BRINGING
BAD NEWS TO
AUTHORITY

In addition to office politics, there was a second dynamic at work as Joseph stood in front of Pharaoh. He was about to bring a devastating message, and some authority figures don't take kindly to bad news. Joseph likely had some insight into how the Pharaoh might react in this situation because he had spent time with two members of his staff, the cupbearer and the baker, when they were in prison two years earlier. Had I been making this presentation, I would likely have had shaky knees and a catch in my throat. But Joseph told it straight, just as he understood it from God.

Perhaps to his surprise, Joseph found that Pharaoh also responded with courage. Rather than fight or dismiss the bad news, he listened carefully not only to Joseph's analysis but to his proposed action as well. We will discuss the plan and what this meant for Joseph in the next two chapters, but it is easy to miss the courage of a leader who receives and acts on bad news. In fact, we read that Pharaoh's officials joined in supporting Joseph's suggestion: "The plan seemed good to Pharaoh and all his officials." This was a great outcome, but it was not guaranteed when Joseph approached Pharaoh, and so it must have been a great relief.

There is a big lesson here. All of us at some time are faced with the question of what to say to someone in authority. The situation is made more difficult when we know that what we have to say is not what they want to hear. It may be tempting to say nothing, out of a desire to protect ourselves. But if we believe that we are called to this position, and are here for a reason, it is important to speak the truth clearly, respectfully, and wisely. This is such an important topic and I want to explore it through multiple examples, both from my own experience and the insight from leaders I have interviewed.

In 2009, while I was doing some work in the Central African Republic, my host and colleague asked me to make a presentation on the problem of corruption to the minister of finance and his staff. At the time, the country ranked among the bottom ten countries in the world on the Corruption Perceptions Index, and the average poverty and lifespan numbers were among the worst in the world. I asked my colleague whether I should tell it straight, or whether I should soft-pedal the bad news. He encouraged me to tell it straight.

I told the finance officials about their ranking in corruption, showed them some data on how corruption is correlated with poverty, and how extreme poverty correlates with poor quality of life. I showed them how global production capacity exceeds demand, and no one is likely to source work to a country they couldn't trust. In short, I told them that if they didn't clean up their act, it would mean a continued sentence of low quality of life for them and for the people in their country. I am certain this was not the message they wanted to hear. I admit I turned to my colleague and asked quietly, "Should I run now?"

To their credit, the minister and his staff responded by asking me to write this up for them; they had never seen most of the data I had presented. It became a positive experience.

In 2002, Sherron Watkins was selected as *Time* magazine Person of the Year in recognition of her role as the whistle-blower at Enron, the energy company that all of Wall Street loved in the late 1990s and early 2000s. The company had piled up an incredible earnings record and *Fortune* magazine named Enron "America's Most Innovative Company" for six consecutive years. But Sherron, a vice president of finance, had uncovered some unsettling news about the company finances and some potentially damaging ways that finances were being handled by the chief financial officer. She needed to make sure company leaders knew about it; therefore, she too had to deliver bad news to someone in authority. Here is her story as she told it for an interview:

> I was working for Andy Fastow [then the chief financial officer of Enron, subsequently in prison] in the summer of 2001. I stumbled across these Raptors [companies not on the Enron books but owned by Enron, "shell companies" that bought Enron products, enabling Enron to post good earnings]. I understood that they were capitalized with Enron stock. I put my family plans on hold. I started interviewing with Enron's competitors in earnest. I just said I have to get out of here. I cannot work for a company that is committing such fraud.
>
> I planned to meet with Jeff Skilling [then CEO] on my last day, when I had a contract with another company. But I will tell you, it was going to be tough to get up the courage to meet him because he was a ruthless "take no prisoners" type of guy. [Skilling himself is still in prison.] I was even worried about it with the safety net of another job. But then he quit, which surprised everyone. The picture of the Titanic came quickly to mind. I was a crew member seeing the water come in, and Skilling's resignation was like the last partition breaking. It was the final piece of evidence that what I was seeing was really bad, and that he knew what was coming.
>
> He quit on a Tuesday, and on Wednesday morning I typed an anonymous letter and sent it to Ken Lay [chairman of the board], knowing that an all-employee meeting was coming up on Thursday. They had a process for looking at these things and I just wanted to float it up there. I went to the all-employee meeting, and Ken Lay was talking about our values: respect, integrity, communication, and excellence. He was the kinder, gentler face of Enron. He got this tremendous standing ovation when he announced that he was stepping back in as CEO. He said that our vision and values had slipped, that we need to get back to them.

And he said if anyone is truly troubled about anything that Enron is doing, please feel free to speak to Steve Kean, Cindy Olson (the head of human resources), or himself. But he didn't say anything about my memo.

I met with Cindy Olson that very afternoon. When I showed her the page I had sent to Ken Lay, she said, "Ken gravitates toward good news. He probably showed this to Rick Causey, the chief accounting officer, and to Andy, and they said there is no basis for concern. So he just threw it away. For him the issue is resolved. But he does better meeting people face to face. Would you be willing to meet with him?" I agreed to identify myself, and set up a meeting with him for the following week. That is about all there was to my thinking process.

Unlike Jeff Skilling, who had abandoned ship, my view was that Ken Lay was an honorable, ethical man. I thought when I told him his ship had a fatal hole, he would check it out. If there was such a hole, he would try to save jobs and business lines, and he would form a crisis management team.

Ken Lay asked executives, as well as Enron advisors, to relook at the plans to make sure we were unsinkable. But nobody went below deck to see if there was a hole. What I put in front of him was one basic question about the Raptor entities that owed Enron a lot of money. How were they going to fund the $500–$700 million in losses? Was it from outside parties, from outside investors or creditors, or was it from Enron stock? If they are going to pay Enron back using Enron stock, I said, then we are done for.

If he had just tried to answer that question and truthfully engage another accounting firm about it, he would not have been able to escape the fact that Enron had committed accounting fraud. But he never looked at that question. He looked at whether I was bringing up anything new. He reassured me that the board knew about the Raptors, that Arthur Andersen had looked at the Raptors. It was bizarre. The CEO has to have pristine ethics, because if there is any erosion in values at the top, it gets magnified in the trenches.[1]

It is easy to see Sherron's fear as she prepared to bring bad news to a boss who didn't like bad news. She put her plans for her family on hold. She found another job. She wrote an anonymous letter. But when she did step up, she found a boss in denial. As already mentioned, Sherron went on to be *Time* magazine co-person of the year (with two other whistle-blowers). Ken Lay died before he went to trial. Many people at Enron lost all of their retirement benefits, and many investors lost a great amount. Enron defined the decade of bad business, and its name has become a term that stands for corporate greed. Sherron, like Joseph, took bad news to someone in authority, but this time the outcome was not positive. Showing the courage to take this step is not always rewarded, but it is the right thing to do.

I had the opportunity to pursue this question through an interview with General Peter Pace, chair of the Joint Chiefs of Staff between 2005 and 2007. His insights on bringing bad news to authority comes from both sides of the question: he has had to bring bad news to his boss, and he has been the boss receiving bad news from a subordinate. First, I asked him how he would disagree with a boss. He replied,

> Very carefully! First of all, I will start by asking questions because this allows you to put a different idea on the table without being directly confrontational. Sometimes, it's just a matter of misunderstanding. If I ask a question, the boss gets a chance to educate me in what he really meant to say. It could be that by asking the question, the boss will realize what he or she is asking you to do is not right. This is a clear victory. Once you have asked enough questions and you are still of the mind that this is wrong, then you can be direct about it, just say, "That's not who I am, I can't do that."
>
> [One time I had to disagree with Defense Secretary Donald Rumsfeld on global television.] To be clear, Secretary Rumsfeld did not give a green light to torturing people at Guantanamo. We spent months with lawyers and judges talking through what we would and would not allow our people to do while interrogating detainees. I was comfortable that the decisions we came up with and the guidance we gave was very much inside the boundaries of what I was

personally comfortable with. This does not mean somebody did not break those rules. But I was very comfortable with the rules.

It was during a press conference that I countered Secretary Rumsfeld in public. Somebody asked the question about "if" an American service person saw torture or abuse of an Iraqi, what should he do? I was not comfortable with the answer Secretary Rumsfeld gave. So I spoke up and I said, "It is the absolute responsibility of every single person in uniform who sees anything that looks like torture, or in any other way sees mishandling of another human being, to do all in your power to stop it." He then said something like, "What General Pace meant is . . ." I countered, "No. I meant what I said."

Press conferences were not my favorite sport. But my mental outlook going in was I was never going to leave a misstatement uncorrected, whether it came from my side or the other side of the microphone. I thought it was important to be very precise on international TV, since millions were watching and there wasn't time for a dialogue between us to gain understanding, which we eventually did. So, I was sad that it ended up being a difference of opinion in public, but I would have been sadder had I not spoken up.

I also asked him for a case in which someone who reported to him brought bad news. Here is what he said:

> There was an event in Vietnam where I almost made a very serious mistake. We had been on a patrol, and a young Marine named Lance Corporal Guido Farinaro, 19 years old, from Bethpage, New York, was killed by a sniper. The bullet came from a nearby village. I was the platoon leader, and he was my machine-gun squad leader. I was enraged, and I called in an artillery strike to get the sniper. Then I looked to my right and saw 21-year-old Sergeant Reid B. Zachary. He did not say a thing, but he simply looked at me, and I knew what I was about to do was wrong.
>
> I called off the artillery strike and we swept the village, as I should have done in the first place. We found nothing but women and children, as the sniper was long gone. I don't know that I could have lived with myself had I done what I originally planned to do. I don't think I would be standing in front of you today. I had almost allowed the rage of the moment to overcome what I

thought was some substantial thinking about who I was going to be in combat.

After the event, I called my platoon together in a little bombed out crater, and I apologized to them. I told them had it not been for Sergeant Zachary, I probably would not have made the right decision. The reaction of the platoon was amazing. It was a very warm, family response, and I learned that a leader admitting mistakes, and thanking those who point them out to him or her, is really important.[2]

General Pace went on to offer some general advice for anyone brought into a situation, as Joseph was by Pharaoh, with a lot on the line: "You should always tell the truth as you know it, and you should understand that there is a whole lot that you don't know. So it is important to have some humility when you are speaking the truth."

I also asked another leader, Alan Mulally, CEO of Ford, how he deals with bad news. He said, "There is no bad news. It is just the way it is. If you don't know it, you can't act on it. So you need to create a climate where you can get any kind of news."

A good leader receives bad news and acts on it appropriately. A poor leader doesn't want to hear bad news. But bad news is always an opportunity to learn and grow. Burying it brings only tougher and more difficult issues when a problem surfaces at a later point.

The challenge is that when you are the bearer of bad news, you don't know which kind of authority figure you will be addressing. Following Joseph's lead and simply speaking the truth (with Peter Pace's qualifier that it should be done with some humility) is good advice, but again we are reminded that it doesn't guarantee the outcome.

13

TALKING ABOUT GOD IN THE WORKPLACE

B usiness and God are like oil and water. They don't mix. Or so goes the "common wisdom" of the twenty-first century. But people of faith often reject the idea of leaving their faith at the door before entering the workplace. How can they handle this delicate intersection of belief and business? Again, when we turn to the life of Joseph, we find remarkable and unexpected insight on this subject.

We see Joseph raising the question of God in three distinct, decidedly secular workplace situations. We will examine each for their applicability to our current world.

The first time this happened was when Joseph was working in the house of Potiphar. When Potiphar's wife tried to persuade Joseph to go to bed with her, he reminded her of his duty to her husband and added, "How then could I do such a wicked thing and sin against God?" (Genesis 39:9). He took a moral stand on the basis of the authority of God in his life. It is not uncommon for Christians to find themselves in a situation where they are encouraged to compromise their own moral stance. The question is how we will deal with this temptation. Joseph's first response to Potiphar's wife dealt with the trust her husband had put in him and his responsibility to be faithful to that trust. But then Joseph raised the bar by not stopping there, recognizing that it would not be a problem just with his boss, but also with God. His response is important, because our moral stance does ultimately go back to God. But we need to be careful how we put this into words as we express our stance in the workplace, recognizing the potential of sounding arrogant and putting down those around us.

In chapter 8 of their wonderful book *Workplace Grace: Becoming a Spiritual Influence at Work* (LeTourneau, 2014), Bill Peel and Walt Larimore discuss the problems Christians sometimes face in dealing with morally challenging situations. Their general advice is that Christians should guard their own moral position while neither embarrassing nor appearing arrogant to those who make other choices. This preserves the opportunity to build the relationships that are so important in the workplace, both personally and professionally. There is a place for a strong and clear statement about God in the midst of a situation, but there are often times when simply turning away from the situation is what is necessary.

The second time Joseph raised the question of God in his workplace was quite different. It had nothing to do with a moral decision; he simply acknowledged God's influence on the insight he was able to offer in the workplace. Joseph did this in two different instances. When he met the two members of Pharaoh's staff in prison, they were worrying that they would never know the meaning of their strange dreams. Offering to help, Joseph told them what they meant: "Do not interpretations belong to God? Tell me your dreams" (Genesis 40:8). Joseph did the same thing after he was brought before Pharaoh. When asked if he could interpret dreams, Joseph responded, "I cannot do it . . . but God will give Pharaoh the answer he desires" (Genesis 41:16).

Taking this position did two things for Joseph. First, it avoided the natural arrogance that can come to those who believe they have unique wisdom. All wisdom comes from God, and acknowledging that fact is both proper and helpful (we will develop this point further in chapter 16). Second, it gave credit to God and acknowledged God's role in Joseph's life. In both of these situations, Joseph gave God the credit for his insight, much as a scholar would credit a source rather than plagiarize.

Some might want to keep God out of any conversation in the workplace, arguing for a strict separation of business and faith. But notice what Joseph did and did not do. He was not proselytizing, telling others that they too must believe in God. He simply identified his own position. Even this can be threatening, however, and needs to be done with care. We should acknowledge God in our work, but again we need to be careful in the way we do it.

A young woman at Boeing was asked by her boss during a staff meeting if she would be able to take on a special project. She responded, "May I pray about it and get back to you this afternoon?" The human resources person pulled her aside after the meeting to tell her that that kind of language in the workplace was out of line. She responded, "Let's just call it diversity, and get over it." The sentiment may be right, but perhaps this is a bit too sarcastic when representing God in the workplace.

With the right amount of caution and attention to others, however, workplace communities can foster conversations about faith. When I was managing a creative group of a hundred and fifty or so scientists, the question of promoting Bible studies, transcendental meditation sessions, political positions, and other generally forbidden topics came up. We pulled together a cross-section of people to draw up guidelines for the open discussion of religion or politics. Both of these subjects had been formally banned from company bulletin boards or other material. The guidelines the group developed were quite simple and required only the application of good judgment:

- Respect others,

- Don't interfere with work,

- Sign and date all postings, and

- Use good taste.

We found that rather than detracting from our work environment, this implementation made people more energized and engaged at work than before. After we had posted these guidelines and subjects on the bulletin board, a visitor to our building commented, "This will get you fired. It will stir up things that have no business in the workplace." But in spite of the dire warning, and the rather vague guidelines, we did not have a single problem over the years I was there.

I would go further. I believe this open expression was an essential ingredient in fostering creativity in our workplace. When people leave a part of themselves at the door, it causes two problems. It would seem to dampen their engagement as a whole person, hence dampening creativity. And if a person's sense of right and wrong is rooted in their religious beliefs, separating their faith and their work can undermine a person's willingness to take ethical decisions at work seriously. In addition, dealing respectfully in this area can help us in dealing respectfully with other differences.

This came back to me when a Jewish person on my staff called me out for participating in a Bible study over lunch in our office. After we talked, he said his primary concern was that I would show favoritism to other Christians. So I asked him to hold me accountable about this, and if he ever saw such favoritism, I would drop out. We met from time to time and built a good friendship that continues long after both of us have left the company. But he made a point that any workplace Christian should think carefully about.

Bob Doll found out the hard way that some work environments don't want the people in their organizations to engage in religious discussion. He was a senior strategist for Black-Rock Capital, a frequent commentator on television, and widely respected. He is also a Christian. During a challenging time at BlackRock, Bob was demoted, and he shared with a group of Christians how he dealt with this difficult period of his life. The talk he gave showed up on YouTube (a problem Joseph did not face!), and he was dismissed for talking about a workplace situation outside of the office. Not long after, he found another position with Nuveen Asset Management, LLC. In the final stages of negotiation for the position, he told his potential new boss about the YouTube videos. The new boss was fine with this, though Bob did not know that would be the case when he raised the issue. It had cost Bob something. Mentioning God in (or related to) the workplace is another area where we are not guaranteed success.

Back to Joseph's stance. Although Joseph was right to attribute his interpretations to God, we need to be careful not to let what should be an expression of humility turn into a way of boosting our own authority. There is a fine line between giving God credit and claiming special insight. The danger here is that we might be tempted to use the claim of having special insight from God to challenge any disagreement with our supposed special revelation. Too often we may want to credit God to win an argument, while God really has nothing to do with our position. A bit of humility is helpful here.

The third time Joseph raised the question of God in his workplace was again different. Joseph also saw others in his workplace as valued human beings; in fact, they too had insight from God. He said to Pharaoh, "The dreams of Pharaoh are one and the same. God has revealed to Pharaoh what he is about to do" (Genesis 41:25). Joseph continued this theme in the ensuing conversation, showing respect to Pharaoh. As a result, Pharaoh acknowledged God's presence and insight in Joseph ("Since God has made all of this known to you . . ."; Genesis 41:39) and entrusted him with great responsibility.

Again, we should offer a word of caution. We would not do this *in order to gain our boss's respect and gain a promotion*. For Joseph, it seemed that this was simply who he was, not a ploy to gain advantage. Further, such conversations do not always, or even often, bring favor from the boss.

The connection between faith and our work remains a challenging one. Rome Hartman, former executive producer for *60 Minutes*, BBC America, and *Rock Center with Brian Williams*, acknowledged that the press also has a difficult time dealing with the subject of religion. He talked about the challenges of handling the issues of faith as a journalist:

> Some news organizations have responded to the [sensitivity of religion] by avoiding the subject to avoid offense. But when you think about the last ten or fifteen years, religious conflict, or conflict that has a religious dimension, has been a huge part of global news. There's been a sharp learning curve. When you think about the way in which people reacted to 9/11, that was the beginning for most Americans of trying to figure out this question. There is definitely a stronger religious component to key events in our world, and we can't duck away from them because they are sensitive or difficult.
>
> Most world religions are dramatically misunderstood by those who are not adherents. There are very few places where people can sit together where it feels safe to talk these things through. There has been an attempt here in Washington, following 9/11, to create a safe place for Christians and Muslims to come together and talk through some of their differences. People retreat to stereotypes pretty quickly if left to their own devices. This is not so much about journalism, but obviously, journalists need to be in there trying to come to a deeper understanding of where faiths affect and shape actions.
>
> Some people now see the need to recognize that we all are informed by what we believe.

He went on to add a personal note on dealing with his own faith in a secular workplace:

> Like most people on a journey, I have come to feel like my Christian faith is more essential to who I am as time's gone along. My professional career and my faith journey have run alongside one another and they intersect more and more. My faith informs who I am, how I treat people, and how I make decisions. It is the foundation for the integrity with which I try to operate. And when I fail, which I do, it affects the way I respond to failure. As I try to be a better man, that process is informed by my Christian faith and hopefully it manifests itself in my work. That may sound simplistic, but it is the way I see it. My job is not to evangelize. It is not my job to try to convert people. In fact it's an important part of my job not to do that, not to put people in a position where they feel that I am exerting pressure or making them feel that they ought to think a certain way. I work for organizations. I did not found my own company. As an employee of an organization, I need to be expressly and properly open to people of every faith.[1]

Bill Pollard, chair and CEO of ServiceMaster, offers insight on this question from the position of the leader of a large, publicly traded company. The company has four values, the first of which is, "To honor God in all that we do." I had the opportunity to ask him about this and how he talked about it in a diverse company with people of many faiths, and no faith.

> In honoring God, we recognized that there is an authority above ourselves for determining right and wrong and that there is a reason for treating every person with dignity and worth—for every person has been created in the image of God. The company did not impose a belief in God, but with this objective, we did raise the question of God. A person's belief in God, or lack thereof, is a personal decision. The company cannot, nor should it, dictate it or define it.
>
> Different people with different beliefs are all part of God's mix. I personally believe that God is involved in all aspects of my life, whether I am in church on Sunday or at work on Monday. I

believe that a person can spend most of his or her life cleaning floors in a hospital or killing bugs in a home, and can grow as a father or a mother, as a contributor to their community, and, yes, even grow in coming to know God. People can take pride in their work as they serve with excellence and, as they do so, they can take pride in themselves. It all wraps together in my mind, and it really reflects what I believe about God. I think God worked when he created this world and he provides work so that we can develop in life, including choosing for him. So seeking excellence in what you do and caring about people, in my view, stems from God.

As a part of our training sessions, we specifically included what it means "to honor God in all we do," and every divisional officer or regional director had to lead one of those sessions. We had pushback from some people about this, and this opened up a discussion on the subject. We used some material in this discussion that was developed by Armand Nicholi, who teaches at Harvard in the medical school. He raises the question of God for his medical students by comparing the worldviews of Sigmund Freud and C. S. Lewis. Both Freud and Lewis addressed the question of God. Both men said that the question of God was the most important question in life. But each man answered the question differently. One said there is no God; and the other said there is God, and I want a relationship with him.

No one should deny the question. It should be resolved on an individual basis and may affect how you ultimately treat people. We promoted an inclusive environment that allowed for diversity of faith and belief but required everyone to treat people with dignity and worth. Over the years, we did not have major legal issues with this position.[2]

Bill offers helpful insight on how he talked about honoring God in a secular company. He collected the talks he had given to his board on the importance and meaning of the company value "Honor God in all we do" in a book titled *Serving Two Masters?* (Delta One Leadership Institute, 2012).

Here is a final important observation to make about Joseph raising the question of God in his workplace. He did excellent work. He was not going around talking about God at the expense of doing his work. While this may be obvious, I have met a number of Christians who believe that God has called them to their workplace to share the gospel with others, and they allow this to distract them from the work they are assigned to do. Or they do enough to get by, but they don't show the level of initiative their work requires. Sometimes they even believe that they are suffering for Christ when they are rated poorly. When doing the work we signed up to do, it is important to do it both diligently and well. Ignoring this is both bad judgment and a poor representation of God. Joseph did his task with excellence and, as we shall see in chapter 27, he saw God's purpose in the work he was doing. His workplace was not simply a platform for talking about God.

14

STRATEGY

When Joseph told Pharaoh the meaning of his dreams, and what he needed to do about the situation, he laid out a strategy for a new business. The fact that this business was a part of the government doesn't change its fundamental nature as a business. Businesses throughout history have been run by the government, though today in the West, most are not. In China in 2005, for example, all of the airlines and oil companies were government run.

As Joseph stood before Pharaoh and his advisors, Joseph was in the same position as a modern-day business consultant. He was there to help his client's business—the Egyptian realm—develop a strategy to meet the coming agricultural situation. His proposal was to set up a new business. Joseph's solution to the problem may seem to come from out of the blue. But if we examine it more closely, we'll find that his proposal follows the same principles that a modern business consultant might use to develop a strategy. He carefully laid out both what the problems were and what needed to be done about them.

If Joseph had an MBA, he would likely have summarized his points in a SWOT analysis. SWOT is a simple diagram that neatly separates the readiness of the team to address the issues (strengths and weaknesses) and the external factors affecting any proposed plan. External factors include both those things outside your control that will help the team (opportunities), and those factors outside your control that could cause you to fail (threats). By honestly identifying these factors, you can then construct a plan to build on your strengths, overcome your weaknesses, take advantage of the situation made available to you through opportunities, and identify clearly how you will avoid being defeated by threats.

I can imagine Joseph stepping up to the whiteboard, marker in hand, and laying out a two-by-two grid. Here is a SWOT Analysis that Joseph might have drawn.

SWOT Analysis
Elements of Strategy based on Pharaoh's Dreams

Availability of farmland *Availability of farmers* *Pharaoh's power to make and* *implement decisions*	*Land of Egypt is large, making* *transportation difficult* *Farmers can be made to work, but* *what about motivation?* *Very long, complex project*
Strengths (internal)	**Weaknesses (internal)**
Seven years of great harvest *starting immediately* *Vastly more grain will be available* *than will be needed* *Know when the famine will be coming*	*Severe famine will start in seven years* *and last seven years* *The Egyptian empire is threated, along* *with Pharaoh's position*
Opportunities (external)	**Threats (external)**

Perhaps he would start by listing the outside threats in the lower right corner: In seven years there will be a famine the likes of which has never been seen. People will die, the empire will likely crumble, and the impact of this will spread to the rest of the world. In the lower left corner, he would list the opportunities: For the next seven years there will be a truly bountiful harvest. The land will be extremely productive. He would then lay out Egypt's strengths: There is lots of land that can be used for planting, there are plenty of farmers, and Pharaoh knows

what is coming. Rather than having to deal with a congress di-
vided over how much the people could be taxed, Pharaoh could
dictate what the people needed to do. Then Joseph might spell
out the country's weaknesses. First, the land of Egypt is large
and transportation is not great. This means that collecting grain
from all of the areas during the plentiful times and distributing
it later will be difficult. Second, the farmers need to be incen-
tivized to work hard during the good years. Too much of a tax
burden may take away their incentive to work hard and slow
the collection of grain. Third, the project will be complicated
and long, lasting fourteen years. There is a need for a leader to
be responsible for management and oversight, and this leader
needs to be one person.

Joseph might have gone on to say that the goal for setting up
this business in Egypt was to turn the weaknesses into strengths,
take advantage of the opportunities, and mitigate the threats.
He might have said that he wanted to take his listeners through
how to deal with the weaknesses and threats, but first he asked
if there were any questions.

Most of his points would have been clear, but we can imagine
that someone might have asked why it was important to have one
person in charge. In twenty-first-century terms, Joseph might
have responded, "An organization, particularly a large organization, run by a committee sounds good until you try it." Generally,
it is simply not a good idea, though it keeps being tried.

There are plenty of modern examples that demonstrate
the importance of the principle Joseph was following when he
recommended that one person lead Egypt's new business. For
example, John Reed was CEO and chair of Citibank when it
merged in 1998 with Travelers Insurance, headed by CEO and
chair Sandy Weill. Although the board decided to make Reed
and Weill co-CEOs, Reed eventually stepped down, leaving Weill
as the sole CEO of the new CitiGroup. Here is the way John reflected on this when we talked with him in 2001:

When it became clear to both Sandy and me that leading together was going to kill CitiGroup (it wasn't that he and I couldn't get along but that the guys working for us were just being driven crazy), I felt strongly that we should both step down to allow a new person to come in from the outside and build a new company. Sandy felt strongly that he should stay on alone for a while and the board said okay. Sandy will retire at some point and it will only be then that the full benefit of the merger will start developing as a new management can begin. Then the emotional turmoil associated with the merged pieces will die.[1]

I could offer many other similar examples of failed attempts at co-leadership in a large organization. Joseph got it right when he advised Pharaoh and his advisors to look for a single leader. Joseph, acting as the consultant, got the problem right according to a modern approach to strategy. He had addressed the first two questions we laid out at the beginning: What is going on and how does this affect us?

The next step for Joseph was to identify how Egypt could capitalize on its opportunities and minimize the external threat, and how to identify what the kingdom could do internally to address its weaknesses and take advantage of its strengths.

The modern consultant would stop before this point to work out a paid contract. My friend Paul runs a strategy and consulting business, and he is always juggling opportunities to develop new projects. He gets paid only after he is under contract, so he must explain enough of his approach to convince potential customers that they should purchase his services—but not so much that they no longer need him. Delivering too much value during the development stage, before the contract is signed, undermines his revenue.

At this point, Joseph went further than most modern consultants would go. He stepped back to the whiteboard to develop the rest of the strategy without a contract. Taking into account Egypt's strengths, opportunities, and threats, he identified a plan for the third weakness on the list. First, he proposed a tax of

20 percent of the harvest. Perhaps he reasoned that the harvests would be so plentiful, people would not miss this much of the grain. They could earn their living, feed their families, and even prosper from 80 percent of a bountiful harvest. Thus he solved the incentive problem. And, he likely reasoned, this would be enough to get the country through the famine.

He also solved the first two weaknesses by proposing the creation of grain collection and distribution centers in different areas of the country. This would minimize the transportation issues, their weakness, both in the collection of the grain and later in the distribution of the grain. The entire plan was based on taking advantages of the opportunities (the bountiful harvest for the next seven years) and the threats (the drought coming in seven years with all of its implications). There were many details that remained to be solved, including staffing, recordkeeping, security, and so on, but he left only one big issue open: How would the project be managed?

Pharaoh and all of his officials loved the whole plan.

Had this been a collaborative discussion in a modern boardroom, at this point Pharaoh would have taken the marker and stepped forward to the whiteboard, saying, "I can solve the project management weakness. Let's have Joseph do this job." He actually said, "Can we find anyone like this man, one in whom is the spirit of God? . . . Since God has made all this known to you, there is none as discerning and wise as you" (Genesis 41:38, 39). Why did he choose Joseph? We see that it was clear to Pharaoh that God was with Joseph and had given him special insight.

Since this was a new project in Egypt, a new government-sponsored multinational corporation, a modern leader might have added that they needed a name and a mission statement for the new company. Without modern naming and branding consultants, they might have come up with a name like the Egyptian International Food Company. And after some discussion, they might have even settled on a mission statement: "We exist to save the world from starvation."

As we can see, Joseph's approach to strategy followed a modern model, and it illustrates what the writer of the book of Ecclesiastes said:

> What has been is what will be, and what has been done is what will be done; there is nothing new under the sun. (Ecclesiastes 1:9)

Or as one more modern writer, Ambrose Bierce (1842–1914), put it:

> There is nothing new under the sun, but there are lots of old things we don't know.

When the economic crisis occurred in 2008, leaders of businesses all over the world, including leaders we meet in this book, convened strategy sessions to discuss how to deal with it. For example, Steve Bell, the owner of Pacific Crest Cabinets, held strategy sessions to try to understand what to do in his business when the building trade ground to a halt. Don Flow, owner of Flow Automotive, called similar sessions to identify a new strategy when auto sales fell 70 percent as fewer people bought cars.

Of course, a strategy session is not just needed in a crisis caused by an external event. Businesses develop strategies for replacing a key leader in the company who has moved on, or for dealing with a new technology. At Apple, Steve Jobs held weekly strategy sessions to look to the future. In one session, he asked what would happen to the iPod as mobile phones became more and more capable. From that session, Apple developed the iPhone, a new market for them.

A new strategy for a business generally requires answering three questions, regardless of the problem being solved:

1. What is going on externally that may impact the business?

2. How does it affect the business?

3. What actions should the business take to survive and thrive?

Each question requires different expertise, and a consultant with special expertise in a particular area is often called in to assess key external factors. In the case of the recession, questions might include:

- How long will the recession last?

- How deep will it go?

At Steve Jobs's strategy session, Apple employees might have asked themselves:

- What is happening in the mobile phone market?

- What products are there and how do they compete with what we are doing?

In the case of the Egyptian International Food Company, Joseph concluded—based on his interpretation of Pharaoh's dream—that the time of plenty would last seven years and the famine would last seven years. He predicted that collecting 20 percent of kingdom's grain would provide enough to get through the famine. These are all planning assumptions, in modern terms, that would need to be validated during the course of the strategy's execution, which we will discuss in chapter 17.

Modern companies facing these questions must ask what all of this means for their business, sometimes with the help of a consultant. This focuses what needs to be done about the situation. But it is not sufficient to have a good assessment. The leadership team has to know precisely what they need to do. Thus they need to assess their own ability to create a new product or develop a service that can help them survive the recession. This might include new people to hire, a company to buy, or costs to cut. Joseph took Pharaoh and his advisors through this as well.

In this chapter, we have been imagining Joseph drafting his solution in a collaborative planning meeting. But although Joseph's strategy bears all the hallmarks of a modern business plan, Scripture tells us that Joseph simply told the plan to Pharaoh and his advisors on the spot. Modern businesspeople can be grateful that they don't have to produce strategic solutions out of thin air the way Joseph did! But there remains the question of how Joseph came up with the strategy he offered to Pharaoh. Certainly, God could have simply revealed the plan to him. (Of course, he can work with people by direct revelation and sometimes does, such as the instructions for building of the tabernacle.) It has been my observation, however, that God generally does not work in this way. Often, instead, he gifts and develops people through experience and study, and provides insight and inspiration more than detailed plans. Joseph, as we saw earlier, had been prepared for business by his father. He had demonstrated the gift of hard and honorable work for Potiphar and while managing the prison. He likely had a great deal of time to think about things in prison as well. And he held firm to his commitment to God. Seen against the backdrop of Joseph's character, even strategic development has spiritual overtones.

There is another puzzling issue to resolve: why did Pharaoh (and his officials) not take advantage of Joseph by simply using his insight and sending him back to prison? They now had enough information to run the project without him.

This kind of thing happens frequently in business today. The leaders will trust the judgment of the consultant in diagnosing the problem and laying out the solution, but then they believe they can implement the solution themselves. After all, what remains is a "simple" matter of carrying out the plan.

Though there is nothing in the text to prove this, I speculate that Pharaoh and his staff saw a high level of risk for anyone who did not have Joseph's insight. What if he was wrong? Would anyone else step forward and risk their life to run a project with this level of uncertainty? Remember, Pharaoh was the absolute ruler. And the stakes were high, not just on a personal basis, risking the wrath of Pharaoh, but on a community basis. On a high-risk, high-importance project, even the biggest of egos may show some fear and deference to choosing the best person for the position.

Now Joseph was out of prison at last. Dramatically so!

15

THE BIG PROMOTION

Pharaoh had decided to make Joseph responsible for leading the Egyptian International Food Company. He had invited Joseph to the discussion based on a single reference from the chief cupbearer. He had observed Joseph in action as he diagnosed the issues facing Egypt and recommended a solution. Filling a position of this level of importance and responsibility would generally call for a search firm and lots of references, but apparently Pharaoh had seen enough. He acknowledged that God was at work in the life of Joseph, and he hired him.

Now, Pharaoh had more decisions to make about his position. What would Joseph's job description be? What would his compensation package look like? And who would he report to in carrying out this work?

From his position of power and authority, Pharaoh might have commanded Joseph to do this job as a slave, reporting to one of his officials. But I think Pharaoh had more insight than this. He saw talent in Joseph that he had not seen in his own officials. He also likely knew that giving someone the responsibility for a job without the authority to do it simply would not work. Interestingly, business leaders struggle with this to this day. So Pharaoh started with the position description and the reporting structure:

> "Since God has made all this known to you, there is no one so discerning and wise as you. You shall be in charge of my palace, and

all my people are to submit to your orders. Only with respect to the throne will I be greater than you." So Pharaoh said to Joseph, "I hereby put you in charge of the whole land of Egypt. . . . I am Pharaoh, but without your word no one will lift hand or foot in all Egypt." (Genesis 41:39–41, 44)

Talk about a promotion! Few people have the opportunity to move from time in prison to a position of such power and responsibility. Then Pharaoh offered Joseph the compensation package and the trappings that went with his new position:

Pharaoh took his signet ring from his finger and put it on Joseph's finger. He dressed him in robes of fine linen and put a gold chain around his neck. He had him ride in a chariot as his second-in-command, and men shouted before him, "Make way!" (Genesis 41:42–43)

All of the resources of the kingdom were now at Joseph's disposal. He had funding for clothes, a company car, and a collection of servants. Pharaoh also provided a wife for Joseph. In terms of title, compensation, authority, and status, Joseph got it all. It is enough to make a twenty-first-century CEO envious.

Perhaps some would have observed this scene, like a gossip columnist of our day, and written about this "overnight success." I like the words of comedian Monty Hall, who once said about himself, "Actually, I am an overnight success, but it took twenty years." It seems that Joseph's hard work finally paid off. He had his dream position. But how does anyone respond to a promotion like this?

It is important not to get too caught up in all this ceremony. The big promotion did bring many opportunities for Joseph, but it also carried an awesome responsibility, to use Bill Pollard's language.[1] He was at the beginning, not the end, of a fourteen-year project that he must bring home successfully. But Joseph seemed to understand this responsibility, as we will explore in the next chapter.

Only a few people I can think of come close to being promoted as dramatically as Joseph was. Nelson Mandela had been in prison in South Africa for many years, and his release in 1991 laid the groundwork for his election as president of the nation in 1994. The difference was that Mandela had effectively been a political prisoner, and his leadership abilities had already been widely recognized.

Two leaders with whom I have met had dramatic promotions as well. I interviewed Hsieh Fu Hua, then the CEO of the Singapore Exchange, and asked him why he had stepped into that powerful position, and what planning and preparation he had had for that work. Here is what he said:

> This opportunity came in a very uncanny way. I had not been in the stock exchange for more than ten years, and never been in this new building. But I came here for personal matters, to settle my mother's affairs as she had passed away three years ago. Just as I walked into this building for the first time, my mobile [phone] rang. The search committee for the new CEO was calling, asking if I would come in for a chat. For the past year I had been feeling that it was time to do something special, but it was a rather unsettling time where I was not sure what that something special would be. So the call to consider the position was uncanny in its timing.

Totally unprepared for such a promotion, Hsieh Fu Hua was simply walking through the building on other business. He had not sought the job, and was just at this time considering the possibility of doing something else. Suddenly, he was in the top spot. As we had tea in his fabulous office in Singapore, he did not talk about the trappings or the title that he had been given. Rather, he focused on the position as an opportunity to do something big, something important:

> I describe it as an artist who has spent years honing his skills experimenting with small portraits. After this comes the opportunity to do a big mural. How then do you resist doing the big

mural? An artist has to express himself. It is the culmination of one's life skills and the desire to realize one's fullest potential. So I call this the big commission.[2]

We will see in the next chapter that this is Joseph's focus as well. For both of these men, the job is about what needs to be done, not the trappings and position that go with it.

Another person who was given a sudden and dramatic promotion is Gloria Nelund, whom we have met before. She had taken an entry-level position at a bank in her hometown in Ohio after college, starting at the bottom of the organization. Through her diligence and hard work, she was promoted to head of operations at that bank, responsible for twenty-five people. What did that hard work look like?

> Early in my career, I adopted three principles that I would follow all of my life: I would work really hard; I would solve problems; and I would help people. I found that I enjoyed making processes efficient, finding a better way to do something. And in the third area, I found joy in making other people successful.

That sounds a bit like Joseph and his hard work in Potiphar's house and in prison. But then Gloria, like Joseph, got a much bigger promotion:

> Not long after that I was offered a head of operations position by a bank in California where just the team I would be managing was 300 people. I had only been to California once when I was twelve, and I was intimidated by the size of the task; but with encouragement, I just went for it. And that got me started in the Bank of America system.[3]

Again, we see in Gloria a focus on the task at hand and a commitment to help others, rather than a focus on position, status, or power.

Not everyone takes this approach to a promotion. There was a young man at Boeing who once asked me to act as a mentor to him. That entailed meeting with him several times over the year, getting to know him, and providing career guidance. For our first meeting, he had filled out a career planning sheet and wanted to talk with me about it. His career goals stated, "My goal is to have your job in ten years, be president of Boeing in twenty, and be president of the United States in thirty years." I remember an awkward silence after he shared this with me. I was completely surprised. I wasn't concerned that he wanted my job, but rather with his approach. I said to him, "Those are just titles. What is it you want to do? What do you hope to accomplish?" He acknowledged he had not thought about that—he simply wanted to achieve certain positions. I told him that was a recipe for disaster, and we proceeded to talk about what kinds of things he was gifted to do and how he could use those gifts to serve others.

Joseph, like Hsieh Fu Hua and Gloria Nelund, now had a new position of responsibility and authority, along with the title and perks to go with the position. The key issue was how he would respond. We will explore that next.

16

DEALING WITH SUCCESS

For a person seeking help in the midst of difficulties and challenges, there are many resources available. Books, articles, and support groups can help in the job search, dealing with illness, and many other types of major life problems. Today, churches sometimes organize prayer around these needs in their congregations. Some people just seem to be naturally good at holding their focus, maintaining their relationship with God, avoiding self-pity, and the like during difficult times, while some require a great deal of support. Joseph seems to have been very much on his own with God during his years as a slave and in prison. We have seen that Joseph is a model for maintaining his focus on God, continuing to understand and do his assignment well, being supportive of his boss, and not spending time in self-pity. We have learned a great deal from his reaction to unjust circumstances.

There seem to be fewer resources available to support someone in times of success. I have never heard a pastor call those who have recently been promoted to come forward for prayer. Yet history will show that at times of peak success, a person is most vulnerable for a fall, in part because it is at this point the person feels self-sufficient, often proud of the good work that elevated them to that position. Joseph was now at the zenith of his career. He had it all going for him. Yet if we read forward in the story, we see little evidence of failing at this point, little evidence that he forgot that he had come to his new position because of the hand of God. Perhaps if we look carefully at what he did, we may see the steps he took for his own protection against success.

In studying this part of the story, I observe that Joseph did three things. First, he remained connected to God. Second, he remained rooted in who he was and found a way to maintain this when he could become self-important. Third, he made a clear distinction between the work he needed to do and the trappings associated with that work. We will look at these areas of Joseph's response to success, comparing him both to those who acted similarly and those who have failed because of success.

Let's start with his connection with God, which involved his understanding of who he was as a person in relationship with God. In the opening two chapters of the Bible, humans (man and woman) were in a garden. They worked together, related to each other, and related to God. All of this was done in the context of God being over all. There was a true sense of integrity to their lives. When sin and brokenness enter the picture in Genesis 3, they were tempted to believe they could be like gods, knowing good and evil without reference to the one true God. In the brokenness of Genesis 3, we see the relationship between the man and the woman, their work, and the worship of God all being damaged. The picture moved from having God at the center to having man at the center. Humans become fragmented people, lacking wholeness.

As I discussed earlier, integrity includes honesty, but it is much more and is best captured by the concept of wholeness. Christ came to bring healing and wholeness to our lives. When Paul says in 2 Corinthians 5 that "God has reconciled us to himself through Christ," I think he is talking about our whole lives, not just our "spiritual" souls. The key to this reconciliation is living our whole lives under God's authority rather than on our own. This includes our work and our human relationships, as well as our relationship with God.

Joseph seemed to do this. We have already seen his acknowledgment of God in his day-to-day work. We do not see him preaching to others or imposing his views on others. He remained rooted in God as his source of meaning.

Gloria Nelund is a modern leader who has taken this to heart. After she had announced her resignation from her position as CEO of the US Private Wealth Management Division of Deutsche Bank, she was asked to give a talk to an organization called Women on Wall Street. Here is what she said:

> I made up a list of things that I had done in my career that I felt were at the root of my success. Number one on the list was daily time with God. It is easy in the hectic pace of business, where you can easily get caught up in the trappings around you, to lose perspective. I find that I need to take time each day to get centered, to gain a larger perspective, and to reconnect with purpose and goals that are bigger than me. Many people think they are too busy to do this, but I have found it essential.[1]

The second thing Joseph did was to root himself in his family. Scripture tells us:

> Pharaoh gave Joseph the name Zaphenath-Paneah and gave him Asenath daughter of Potiphera, priest of On, to be his wife. . . . Before the years of famine came, two sons were born to Joseph by Asenath daughter of Potiphera, priest of On. Joseph named his firstborn Manasseh and said, "It is because God has made me forget all my trouble and all my father's household." The second son he named Ephraim and said, "It is because God has made me fruitful in the land of my suffering." (Genesis 41:45, 50–52)

A family can keep us grounded in the midst of our success because we are not a part of that family because of our success. The family connects with us because of our relationships with one another, not because of our successes or failures. Others may offer praise or overstate our accomplishments, perhaps with the thought of finding an inside track to become a part of our success. Not our kids! The daily chores cannot be skipped just because of a great accomplishment at work. My dad used to remind me that even famous people put their pants on one leg at a time.

It is also critical to continue to do the ordinary things of life. I was once in Ukraine with a team of people, teaching basic business principles to people who had significant economic needs. At the conclusion of the conference, we were asked to wait in the hall while the group gathered, and then we were brought into the auditorium to sit on the platform and answer final questions. As we came in, the people stood and cheered. As we looked out at that crowd, gratified that God had blessed our work, I said to the person next to me, "When I get home, I will still have to take out the garbage." We need to find a way to remind ourselves that we belong in a much bigger context. We are ordinary people not defined by our successes.

Marshall Carter, former chair and CEO of Cleveland Street Bank, talked in an interview about how he dealt with the potential isolation factor as a CEO:

> When you are successful as a CEO it is really hard to keep your feet on the ground. You have got to do a lot of management by walking around, talking to the different employees, getting many different views—even negative ones.
>
> Because I have been a pilot for almost 25 years now, I keep my plane down at a little airport. They do not really know who I am, just another guy with an airplane. I talk with the guys in the hanger, the guys pumping gas, and you can connect with real people. A lot of these CEOs are isolated. They only see other CEOs. I have never once gone to one of these CEO things over the weekend because I want to avoid that isolation factor.[2]

I have had to learn the hard way about dealing with my own pride. One of the worst falls I ever took while skiing is a painful reminder. I had come off some difficult terrain at Sun Valley and was feeling good about the way I was skiing. The slope was leveling off as I approached the lift, and I remember thinking to myself, "I am really skiing well today." I have no idea what happened at that moment, but I suddenly found myself face-planted in the snow, goggles, hat, and gloves strewn down the hillside in full view of those starting up the chairlift. This moment has been a good reminder every time I think I am doing well in another aspect of life.

For some, failing the challenge of success has been played out visibly before a much larger audience. In 2009 Tiger Woods, an internationally acclaimed golfer and celebrity, was near the peak of his game and career. But in early 2010 a number of affairs came to light. His failures were front-page headlines and lead stories on the news. His personal and professional lives have never recovered. When he confessed to his adulterous relationships, he said, "I knew my actions were wrong but I convinced myself that normal rules didn't apply. . . . I felt that I had worked hard my entire life and deserved to enjoy all the temptations around me. I felt I was entitled."[3] There couldn't be a clearer picture of the dangers of success. People can begin to believe that their abilities and the position they've attained are all of their own doing. Normal rules no longer apply.

Tiger Woods was not alone in finding failure at the pinnacle of success. The Bible tells us of many similar failures. Consider, for example, the case of Uzziah the king of Judah:

> Uzziah provided shields, spears, helmets, coats of armor, bows and slingstones for the entire army. In Jerusalem he made devices invented for use on the towers and on the corner defenses so that the soldiers could shoot arrows and hurl large stones from the walls. His fame spread far and wide, for he was greatly helped until he became powerful. But after Uzziah became powerful, his pride led to his downfall. He was unfaithful to the LORD his God. (2 Chronicles 26:14–16)

Apparently, Uzziah also took on the feeling of entitlement.

The same destructive behavior can happen to companies. In his book *How the Mighty Fall: And Why Some Companies*

Never Give In, noted business writer Jim Collins identifies five factors in the failure of once-great companies. The first step ("Stage 1") he discusses is "Hubris Born of Success":

> Great companies can become insulated by success. Stage 1 kicks in when people become arrogant, regarding success virtually as an entitlement, and they lose sight of the true underlying factors that created success in the first place. . . . Luck and chance play a role in many successful outcomes, and those who fail to acknowledge the role luck may have played in their success—and thereby overestimate their own merit and capabilities—have succumbed to hubris.[4]

Joseph also illustrates a third way of protecting himself against failure due to pride at the time of success. In addition to depending on God and being rooted in the ordinary things of his life, Joseph must have looked forward to the long and arduous task ahead of him. He had not been given his promotion to sit back and enjoy the perks of his position, but rather to carry out the fourteen-year project of providing food for the world. As obvious as this is, it is easily overlooked, as many forget about the challenges ahead. Take the time to celebrate, but then get back to work.

Success is often associated with a time of celebration—but as we have seen, it is also a time of vulnerability. The life of Joseph has shown us three ways to remain rooted in times of success: keeping our perspective on who we are before God, who we are in relationship to those around us, and the work we have been given to do. Together these things constitute a life of integrity. We get into trouble when we try to separate them.

Ray Kroc, founder of McDonalds, illustrates this separation: "I believe in God, family, and McDonald's and, in the office, that order is reversed." I believe both of Kroc's orders are wrong. Such a linear order suggests separate categories and a lack of integrity. Rather, if God is our only priority, and we see our families and our work as a part of that life under God, it changes the way we think about our family and our work. Both are a part of our service to God.

Jesus talked about this attitude of service with his disciples:

> "You know that those who are regarded as rulers of the Gentiles lord it over them, and their high officials exercise authority over them. Not so with you. Instead, whoever wants to become great among you must be your servant, and whoever wants to be first must be slave of all. For even the Son of Man did not come to be served, but to serve, and to give his life as a ransom for many." (Mark 10:42–45)

Joseph models the unity of life that can be so troublesome for the rest of us. He demonstrated integrity in his life. And he saw the challenge of the task he had been given and focused his energy on doing it well. He was also rooted in God and in his family. In this sense there is no difference between the work of Joseph and our work in the twenty-first century.

17

EXECUTING THE STRATEGY

In the 1972 film *The Candidate,* Robert Redford's character goes through all of the rigors of a political campaign, dealing with travel, sleepless nights, endless speeches, ultimately resulting in victory at the polls. He wins. But in the closing scene of the movie, he is sitting on the side of the bed speaking with his campaign manager and says, "Marvin, what do we do now?" It's easy to get caught up in winning the position, whether in politics or business, and forget that it is just the starting point.

Joseph has emerged from prison, been selected to do the job as the Chief Executive Officer of the Egyptian International Food Company, and been through the wonders of his inauguration and the introduction to his new life. The band has stopped playing, and it is time to get to work. The strategy that he laid out is in place, but now that strategy must be executed.

"Strategy execution has always been one of the more difficult problems in business. Creating a brilliant strategy is nothing compared to executing it successfully," writes Thomas Davenport, professor and noted business author in his December 6, 2007, blog post. I appreciate the way Melissa Raffoni put it in her Harvard Management Update (February 26, 2008): "Strategic planning gets all the cachet and all the ink, but the most creative, visionary strategic planning is useless if it isn't translated into action."

Why is execution so much more difficult than planning? The strategic planning process is creative, energizing, and focused. Joseph laid out the strategy for the work ahead in a short time. The execution of that strategy would take fourteen years.

Here is a small sample of the kinds of situations Joseph would need to manage. He would probably spend most of his time dealing with small matters. For example, perhaps everyone has an assignment but one person gets sick. Or perhaps he assumed he would need five clerks at the collection center but the grain arrived at one time, requiring ten people to log it in. There would be some bigger issues as well. Someone had to hire and train the people needed in the process. Joseph needed to establish a culture so that if something went wrong in the process, people would be willing to make it known without fear of reprisal. In addition, Joseph must validate his initial assumptions and change them if necessary. For example, was the 20 percent tax on grain during the good years the right amount? Did he properly interpret the dream regarding the length of the time of plenty or the length of the famine?

On top of all of these things was the endless business travel necessary to organize the grain collection throughout the entire kingdom. At the end of his initial commissioning we read, "Joseph went out from Pharaoh's presence and traveled throughout Egypt" (Genesis 41:46). Sure, it was probably first-class travel, but it would have been tiring nonetheless.

In one of the few excellent books on the subject of execution strategy, *Execution: The Discipline of Getting Things Done*, authors Larry Bossidy and Ram Charan write:

> Don't confuse execution with tactics. Execution is a systematic process of rigorously discussing hows and whats, questioning, tenaciously following through, and ensuring accountability. It includes making assumptions about the business environment, assessing the organization's capabilities, linking strategy to operations and the people who are going to implement the strategy,

synchronizing those people and their various disciplines, and linking rewards to outcomes. It also includes mechanisms for changing assumptions as the environment changes and upgrading the capabilities to meet the challenges of an ambitious strategy.[1]

Scripture doesn't tell us exactly what steps Joseph followed in executing his strategy, although we do get glimpses of it along the way. Modern-day business practices suggest execution over a long time period requires three components, given the following strategy:

1. A motivating vision that keeps the goal in mind;

2. A careful, adaptable plan in which everybody knows their part;

3. Strong determination to carry out the work, particularly during tough times or when the project has lost its excitement.

I can picture Joseph using a motivating vision throughout the project when the work got hard, whether it was gathering the food or distributing it. He would remind his team of their company mission: "We exist to save the world from starvation."

In the back of his mind, although he surely realized that God was with him, Joseph must still have feared that if he did not deliver, he could go the way of the chief baker. His personal future was at stake—and the rewards were potentially significant if he was successful. But he must also have known that the material rewards were not the most effective motivation for himself or his team. In *Built to Last: Successful Habits of Visionary Companies*, Jim Collins and Jerry Poras talk about the way the best companies motivate their people: through what they call BHAGs (Big Hairy Audacious Goals).[2] Accomplishing something that makes a difference is more important than personal wealth or fear of failure. That recognition made one of my experiences at Boeing quite painful.

We had one president at Boeing who tried to inspire a group of us at an executive retreat to face the challenge of the coming year. He told the story of how wealthy he was, and how important it was for all of us to keep our eyes on the goal of making more and more money. He didn't say anything about our great products and what they would mean for the world. I was not the only one who came away from that session completely discouraged about that difficult phase of corporate life.

Joseph was managing a BHAG, to borrow from Collins and Poras! Joseph's project was bigger in scope and scale than most major projects today. It called for endurance, persistence, and adaptation along the way. Here is the description of the project in the text:

> During the seven years of abundance the land produced plentifully. Joseph collected all the food produced in those seven years of abundance in Egypt and stored it in the cities. In each city he put the food grown in the fields surrounding it. Joseph stored up huge quantities of grain, like the sand of the sea; it was so much that he stopped keeping records because it was beyond measure. . . . The seven years of abundance in Egypt came to an end, and the seven years of famine began, just as Joseph had said. There was famine in all the other lands, but in the whole land of Egypt there was food. When all Egypt began to feel the famine, the people cried to Pharaoh for food. Then Pharaoh told all the Egyptians, "Go to Joseph and do what he tells you." (Genesis 41:47–49, 53–55)

The execution through the first seven years seemed to go flawlessly. Grain came in as promised and was collected successfully. Joseph needed processes to take in the grain, record the amounts, and make sure that each person delivered what was owed. We see him adapting his process along the way, as stated in Genesis 41:49: "Joseph stored up huge quantities of grain, like the sand of the sea; it was so much that he stopped keeping records." Without modern information processing capability, it was simply not possible to keep up the records of how much grain they were receiving. But the collection was so successful that the records no longer seemed necessary. A large pile of grain may seem like enough until distribution time comes. This decision was a much bigger decision than it looks to be.

We don't see the process Joseph went through for hiring and rewarding the people at each location, but because the project was successful, we can assume this was done well. Another important step in the execution of a large-scale project is to lay out the work in such a way that each person's part of the work will fit together. For a large project this requires consistent work processes that are reliably carried out the same way every time. This can also be frustrating for individual workers who might see a better way to do something, without the insight of how that improvement will affect another person's work. We know little of how Joseph did this. To understand something of the scope of this challenge, we consider a modern-day example of the Ford Company.

Alan Mulally also faced a large-scale production problem when he became the CEO at Ford in 2006. Like other automotive companies in the United States, Ford had been faltering both in strategy and execution. Mulally initially put a great deal of time into changing the Ford strategy. They eliminated the brands that were not a part of Ford and started to build cars again. They had a strategy to create a family of new cars around the world, and to make these cars from parts common to various models and designs in different parts of the world.

He also had to create a production plan, or execution plan, that required better coordination than they had ever had before. So he instituted a weekly review for every program in Ford, in which everyone shared their progress with everyone else and every division leader reported on progress toward the goal. The report included the status of product development, staffing, finances, manufacturing rates, and much more. To do all of this within a reasonable time, he used "stoplight" charts with each category shown in green, yellow, or red. Green meant things were on track, yellow signified a problem that was under control, and red was a problem that was not under control. To avoid getting bogged down, they didn't try to solve problems in the meeting but simply to identify those people who could help create the solution—with the mission always in mind. Here is how he described these meetings:

> Every Thursday, 320 slides, two hours and fifteen minutes. Everybody knows everything that is going on. We have a very clear statement at the top of this dog-eared piece of paper I carry with me everywhere: "People working together as a global enterprise for automobile leadership."

Mulally had some tools that enabled him to bring people together and share common data each week that Joseph did not have. But the key point is that he was both enthusiastic and relentless in getting people engaged and ensuring that they were making progress toward the goal.

A key factor in carrying out one of these large-scale projects is to develop "standard processes" for efficiency. Much of this dates back to Henry Ford and the automobile assembly line. Early in the company's history, Henry Ford made a famous statement about the difficulty of using standard processes. "Why," Ford asked in exasperation, "when I only want to hire a pair of hands, do I get a whole person?" So I asked Mulally how he viewed execution today.

> I think the reason Henry Ford said that was that he also was the one that perfected the moving line. Everybody had a location and a job to do, and to make it work there could be no deviation. He hadn't figured out the continuous quality improvement methodology of the Japanese.
>
> It is not that Ford was trying to make you a robot, but you are supposed to be a reliable worker. That means don't freelance, because then production breaks down. That's where that

came from, but now we have the best of both worlds because we execute and still innovate. You have that small incremental continuous improvement where you want everybody's hearts and minds, not just their hands. Then for your new design team you collect all of the product improvement ideas and incorporate them on the next vehicle. [3]

Mulally was so successful in leading Ford that *Fortune* magazine rated him as one of the top three leaders in the world in 2014 and the highest-ranked business CEO. No doubt Joseph would have been there with him in the rankings had *Fortune* been doing their rankings in that day. Joseph faced challenging execution problems many years ago that were not that much different from what Mulally faced: juggling lots of things at the same time, adapting to changing conditions, and keeping people engaged and energized all at the same time. It might seem that with slave labor, there is no problem with keeping people engaged, since they have no choice. But whether a slave or a "wage slave," engagement is still vital. You can make someone work, but you can't make that person work efficiently or wisely. Mulally understood this, and I believe Joseph did as well. We will see in later chapters that Joseph's willingness to communicate was an important part of his management style.

The problem gets more challenging when we come to the distribution part of Joseph's plan.

When the famine had spread over the whole country, Joseph opened all the storehouses and sold grain to the Egyptians, for the famine was severe throughout Egypt. And all the world came to Egypt to buy grain from Joseph, because the famine was severe everywhere. (Genesis 41:56–57)

There had been a hint in the plan that the famine would be widespread, but now Joseph needed to deal with providing grain for the world well beyond the borders of Egypt. Such an adaptation is not unusual. In fact, I have never been on a large project that did not have some significant changes along the way, whether a large airplane design program or the implementation of a large computer system.

More adaptations to the plan, however, would be required. The country did not run out of food, as might have been anticipated, but the people coming to buy grain ran out of money. In chapter 21, "Fairness and Justice," we will see how Joseph adapted his plan to deal with this unexpected situation.

People of faith may view the subject of executing business strategies as part of the ordinary things of life, totally separated from anything spiritual. But much of the Bible is devoted to reminding us of the importance of working at the little things and doing them well. John makes this point, admonishing, "Dear children, let us not love with words or speech but with actions and in truth" (1 John 3:18). And James writes, "Someone will say, 'You have faith, I have deeds.' Show me your faith without deeds, and I will show you my faith by my deeds" (James 2:18).

We may be tempted to spiritualize these texts by applying them only to the so-called spiritual work we do. But certainly these "deeds" and "actions" include our daily tasks. We may also want to limit this biblical exhortation to acting ethically or treating other people fairly. This, too, is important, but it is not the whole picture. I believe that what John and James are saying extends to the spiritual importance of all the work we do—whether designing a new product, creating a sales strategy, or executing a business plan.

Joseph seemed to take this approach, carrying out his work in a way that honored God, and not just for Pharaoh or his own agenda.

18

A Troubling Customer

Suddenly, there they were. It had to be them. Those ten scraggly looking men in line to buy food must be the brothers who had sold Joseph into slavery twenty years ago. What a range of emotions must have gone through Joseph's head as he contemplated this thought! Curiosity. *I wonder how they are doing? Where is my younger brother Benjamin? Is my father still alive?* Anger. *That painful day was more than half my lifetime ago, and I still can't get over it. I thought I was done with that family. I even named my first son Manasseh, "God has made me forget all my trouble and all my father's household," because I thought I was done with that dysfunctional family.* Revenge. *I knew I had created that sign "We reserve the right to refuse service to anyone" for a reason. Do I have to supply them with food?* Uncertainty. *How do I handle this? What if they recognize me? How should I approach them?*

Joseph was seventeen when his brothers sold him into slavery. He was thirty-seven when the famine began and when his brothers arrived shortly thereafter. He looked like an Egyptian, had learned the language, and was surrounded by servants. So there was a good chance his brothers would not recognize him.

The easy response, and one that many businesses today use, would be to simply refuse to work with these troubling customers. Send them on their way. Joseph had already closed that chapter of his life and had a big job to do. He didn't need this. But what seemed to dominate Joseph's response was the question: Have they changed? Are they sorry for what they did? Can I trust them now? Is there any hope to rebuild this broken relationship?

While business may seem to an outsider to be unemotional, strictly governed by the laws of economics and exchange, nothing could be further from the truth. Business is conducted between people, whole people. And at the heart of any transaction between real people is the presence or absence of trust. Complex business deals, in the presence of trust, can be sealed with nothing more than a handshake. Without trust, detailed contracts and teams of lawyers must be present to protect the interests of both sides. Every contingency must be analyzed, anticipated, and documented to assure protection under all circumstances. Francis Fukuyama develops this case in his book *Trust: The Social Virtue and the Creation of Prosperity*.[1]

What brought Joseph's brothers to Egypt? Back in Canaan, Jacob had gone to his sons and said, "Why do you keep looking at each other? . . . I have heard that there is grain in Egypt. Go down and buy some" (Genesis 42:1–2). Apparently, none of Joseph's brothers had yet stepped up to take responsibility for their own future.

"When Joseph's brothers arrived, they bowed down to him with their faces to the ground" (Genesis 42:6). Another dream fulfilled! "He pretended to be a stranger and spoke harshly to them. 'Where do you come from?' he asked. 'From the land of Canaan,' they replied, 'to buy food.' . . . Joseph said, 'You are spies! You have come to see where our land is unprotected'" (Genesis 42:7, 9). The brothers quickly retorted: "Your servants are honest men, not spies! . . . [We] were twelve brothers, the sons of one man, who lives in the land of Canaan. The younger is now with our father, and one is no more" (Genesis 42:10, 12). At this point Joseph knew they were telling the truth, that they had not forgotten him, that Benjamin was all right, and that his father was still alive. Joseph had a tremendous advantage in this conversation. Although he spoke through a translator, he understood what his brothers were saying. Joseph challenged them to go back to Canaan to get their brother and return to prove their story, and when they said they couldn't do that, he had them put in prison for three days. After three days he modified the deal: he would keep Simeon, one of his brothers, in prison in Egypt and the rest could return with their food to feed their families. Simeon would be released when they brought back their brother Benjamin. In the course of these hostage negotiations, the brothers concluded that they were being punished for what they had done to Joseph twenty years earlier, and they argued over who was most responsible for the deed. Hearing this, Joseph had to step aside so they could not see him weep.

As the nine brothers returned home to their father without Simeon, they stopped to rest and were horrified to find that the money they had used to buy food was still in the tops of their sacks. Scripture says that "their hearts sank and they turned to each other trembling and said, 'What is this that God has done to us?'" (Genesis 42:28). Unbeknownst to them, Joseph was continuing to test his brothers.

When they returned to Jacob, he too was frightened and upset. He insisted that they could not take Benjamin with them, and so they lived off the food they had purchased and Simeon remained in prison in Egypt. But when the food ran out, it became necessary for them to return to Egypt. At first Jacob resisted, but the brothers said they could not return to Egypt without Benjamin, and Judah stepped forward with a promise of safety for Benjamin. Jacob had no choice: "May God Almighty grant you mercy before the man so that he will let your other brother and Benjamin come back with you. As for me, if I am bereaved, then I am bereaved" (Genesis 42:14).

When they arrived back in Egypt and came before Joseph with double the money and gifts, he saw they had done as he had requested by bringing Benjamin, so he invited them to a feast at his home. But once again, Joseph had to leave them because of his tears at seeing "his own mother's son" (Genesis 43:29). Following Egyptian custom, Joseph was seated at his own table and the brothers were seated separately. But Joseph continued to play mind games with them. He had them seated in birth order at their table and provided Benjamin with five times the portions of the others.

While their grain was being packaged for the return trip, Joseph instructed his steward to again return their money to their sacks, but this time to put his own silver cup in Benjamin's sack. After they had received their grain and started to return home, Joseph had his steward go after them and ask them why they had repaid his kindness to them with evil. He charged them with stealing his silver cup. The brothers denied the charges, adding, "If any of your servants is found to have it, he will die, and the rest of us will become my lord's slaves" (Genesis 44:9). During the search of their bags, "the cup was found in Benjamin's sack. At this, they tore their clothes" (44:13).

When they returned to the city, they threw themselves to the ground before Joseph. "What is this you have done?" Joseph asked. "Don't you know a man like me can find things out by divination?" (44:15). Judah, stepping up to a leadership position for truth—perhaps for the first time in his life—took the lead. He said to Joseph, "How can we prove our innocence? God has uncovered your servants' guilt" (44:16). When Judah told Joseph that they would all become his slaves, Joseph replied, "Far be it from me to do such a thing! Only the man who was found to have the cup will become my slave. The rest of you, go back to your father in peace" (44:17).

The old Judah, who thought only of himself and who had the original idea to sell Joseph into slavery, would have done just this. But now he proceeded to tell Joseph the story of their discussion with their father and how they negotiated to bring

Benjamin with them. He concluded the discussion by saying that returning without Benjamin would kill their father with grief. He therefore stepped forward with an offer of his own: "Please let your servant remain here as my lord's slave in place of the boy, and let the boy return with his brothers. How can I go back to my father if the boy is not with me? No! Do not let me see the misery that would come upon my father" (44:33–34).

Apparently Judah's self-centered behavior of the past was gone, and the older brother was ready to sacrifice his own life for Benjamin's for the sake of his father. Someone other than Judah mattered to Judah. This was the clincher for Joseph, the words for which he had been waiting. He broke down and wept openly. Then he sent all of his servants out from their gathering and revealed himself to his brothers.

They "were terrified at his presence" when they realized who they were speaking to. But Joseph, now able to trust his brothers and even forgive them, immediately tried to put these fears to rest by putting the situation into perspective in a beautiful speech of reconciliation:

> "Come close to me. . . . I am your brother Joseph, the one you sold into Egypt! And now, do not be distressed and do not be angry with yourselves for selling me here, because it was to save lives that God sent me ahead of you. For two years now there has been famine in the land, and for the next five years there will be no plowing and reaping. But God sent me ahead of you to preserve for you a remnant on earth and to save your lives by a great deliverance. So then, it was not you who sent me here, but God." (Genesis 45:4–8)

Joseph brought healing, not just to his relationship with his brothers, but perhaps for the first time to his relationship with himself. Now he could see a clear purpose for all of the events in his life, and it changed him as well as his relationship to his brothers. It's important to notice that even though he had already reached the pinnacle of success in Egypt, Joseph's own achievement was still somehow incomplete until he was able to be reconciled to his brothers and realize that his work had been for his family all along. The biblical story shows us that Joseph's success wasn't just measured by how much he could rise to personal greatness despite the people who hurt him and tried to extinguish his dreams. Instead, Joseph was successful when he reconciled his work with his once-hateful brothers.

He then told them to go back and get his father and to bring him and all the family to wait out the famine in Egypt. And when word got back to Jacob, he said, "I'm convinced! My son Joseph is still alive. I will go and see him before I die" (Genesis 45:28).

This powerful family drama plays out in the middle of our business story. Is it a distraction, or is it central? In my view, this dimension of the story is right at the heart of any business. Businesses are carried out by people, whole people. What happens in the family affects life at work. I will never forget the time when a scientist on my research staff at Boeing came to tell me that his daughter had been diagnosed with leukemia. It was a devastating time for him, and we needed to make allowances for his time away during this difficult period.

This encounter between Joseph and his brothers leads to valuable insights that go well beyond family relationships. The first concerns the relationship between a business and its customers. Peter Drucker famously said, "The purpose of business is to create and keep a customer." More in the folklore of business is, "The customer is always right." There is no business without customers. But businesses have a much more complicated relationship to their customers than these statements suggest. Good business leaders sometimes have to think of the majority of their customers rather than the minority.

Jeff Pinneo, former CEO of Horizon Airlines (part of the Alaska Airlines system), told this story about his company. Alaska Airlines had grown by moving people through the back country of Alaska. The leaders of the airline developed a culture that would wait for a passenger, never wanting to leave someone who had been delayed. But as the airlines grew into a large national carrier, they found this culture didn't serve them or their passengers well. By waiting for one customer, they might cause eighty to miss a connection. They had the worst on-time record of any national carrier. They recognized that sometimes to serve all customers they must be willing to leave one customer who is late. Starting with this realization, Alaska Airlines had to change the way it did business and moved from last to first in on-time performance. They came to realize they had been catering to one person and having a negative impact on many, and they couldn't run a business that way.

Another insight we can glean from this episode in Joseph's life is the role of trust in a business relationship. While Joseph had a personal reason for working out the problem of trust in his relationship with his brothers, this is a common business need as well. The trust that is needed must go two ways. The business must find trustworthy customers, and the customers must deal with trustworthy businesses. Joseph's trickery, particularly around the incident of planting the cup in Benjamin's sack, raises another important question: Is trickery and deceit at the heart of good business practice after all? And how does that fit with trust? We explore this question in the next chapter.

Yet another issue deals with the role of fear and forgiveness in business. We see fear in Joseph's brothers' reaction to him, and we later see fear when the people start running out of money and need food. In chapter 20 we will look at the role of fear and forgiveness in business using the model of Joseph and some modern-day examples.

There is no business without a customer, and anyone in business must learn how to handle challenging situations with customers.

19

TRANSPARENCY, HONESTY, AND INTEGRITY

The Joseph we have seen interacting with his brothers seems very different from the Joseph we saw when he was seventeen. Then, he was straightforward in telling his dreams to his brothers and his father—straightforward to the point of being some combination of naive and arrogant. Even when Joseph emerged from prison to meet with Pharaoh and tell him the meaning of his dreams, he acted in a straightforward way, almost to a fault. He not only shared all that he knew about the meaning of the dreams, but he went on to lay out a proposed plan that others might have picked up and implemented, sending him back to prison. Throughout the execution of his strategy, through the collection and distribution of grain, there is no indication that he used any form of dishonesty to execute the business plan.

What happened to Joseph in the relationship with his brothers? His interactions with his brothers are characterized by deceit and trickery. Here Joseph's business dealings seem to reflect the way his father Jacob had done business. Deceit and trickery had been the tools Jacob used to build his fortune. Are we to conclude therefore that in business, deceit and trickery are indeed the norm? Or are we to conclude that Joseph was out for revenge and used his dishonesty to achieve it?

To start with, let's draw some distinctions among transparency, honesty, and integrity. *Transparency* is being completely open. Every action and thought I have is available for others to see. While *honesty* is about telling the truth, *integrity* is a bit different. As we discussed earlier, integrity is about wholeness. It includes bringing the whole context into play, seeing the situation in a bigger frame. It may include identifying situations in which transparency, or even honesty, may be inappropriate. Joseph was transparent when he told his dreams to his brothers or flaunted the special coat his father had made him in front of them. But this had proven to be unwise.

In his book *Bribery and Corruption*, Malaysian Methodist bishop Hwa Yung discusses this in the context of the corruption and bribery that are rampant in so many parts of the world today:

> God's various moral commands are absolute, but they are not all at the same level of importance. To tell a lie in order to save a life in certain (and not just any) circumstances is to recognize that life-saving is more important than truth-telling in God's hierarchy of values. This does not mean that lying is right in and of itself.[1]

In Joseph's case, there were two important factors at play. First, he did not see his brothers as trustworthy, which affected his interactions with them. As author and ethicist David Gill writes, "Trust requires trustworthiness. I can't have a trusted relationship with someone who is known to be untrustworthy."[2] Second, Joseph had a larger goal for his relationship with his brothers. He didn't want to leave the relationship in its broken state, so he wanted to test them to see if they might be trustworthy.

Another point to focus on here is that Joseph's actions toward his brothers focused on testing them, not on gain for himself or for his business. This reminds me of the pastor of a large church who went to the bank on Monday morning. He counted the money the teller had passed to him and found there was an extra ten dollar bill. When he pointed this out, the teller replied, "I know. I was just testing. I was in church yesterday and wanted to see if what you said on Sunday is what you did on Monday."

The idea of acting with wholeness or integrity carries with it the opportunity to deceive ourselves if we selectively tell the truth, or to rationalize a justification for acting deceitfully. It is certainly not often the case that we should simply tell a lie to attain a better outcome. The Apostle Paul warns us against this: "Why not say—as some slanderously claim that we say—'Let us do evil that good may result'? Their condemnation is just!" (Romans 3:8).

As he matured, Joseph seemed to navigate the rocky waters of transparency, honesty, and integrity quite well. As modern business leaders face the same challenge, we will now look at the way three individuals have tried to address this same issue. First, I will introduce these leaders who have developed their own approaches to transparency in business dealings, and then I will compare their approaches with that of Joseph.

Jack vanHartesvelt negotiates large real estate contracts in building hotels and resorts across the U.S. In my interview with him, he told me: "One day I had an epiphany about the traditional approach to negotiations. I realized that typical negotiations are based on lies. If I want to get a 3 percent fee, I would tell the other side that I absolutely must have 4 percent, recognizing that they are going to have to drag me down to 3 percent to feel like they 'won,'" he said. But in 1992, he decided he no longer wanted to do negotiations in the standard way.

> Part of this came from a bad experience I had had, where I really took advantage of someone—completely legally. But I didn't like the result. The second part came from my faith—there was this dissonance between what I believed in that part of my life, and what I did in the rest of my life.

He concluded, "I think there is a fair deal out there for everybody," and told the lawyers on his negotiating team, "I want to actually make sure everybody gets what they bargain for. I am not going to say I want something when I don't really want it. I don't want someone's legitimate interests to be undermined."

The lawyers told me I couldn't do that. The board of directors expected me to put these projects together for our benefit, only protecting the interests of our company. They said they wouldn't work with me unless I got permission from the board to amend the approach. In fact, the board didn't realize all of the twisting and turning that went into a typical contract negotiation, and to their credit they just said, "Yes. Those are actually our values, too." I do not think they realized how hard it is to do that sometimes.

The first negotiation I did after that was for a project in the South with two real estate developers who were really struggling due to an economic downturn. They had lost some of their properties; others were embattled. They were locked in unpleasant confrontation with bankers, lawyers, and partners. It was a very difficult time for them. I walked in and said, "Here is the way I want to do the deal. I want this to be a deal that is good for both of us, so I will look out for you and I want you to look out for me." They looked at me skeptically and said, "Right, sure."

Early in the negotiation I said, "If you turn to page 3, section 1.2.5, it says your development fee is 3 percent, but if you go over the development agreement here, it says that if you are ever in default for any reason, you can never recover your fee. I think that could deprive you of what you actually earned, so I would like to change this provision here or that provision there so that I cannot legally take away what was rightfully yours."

They laughed uneasily, but of course agreed to the change. A little further in the negotiations, I pointed out another combination of provisions that could be bad for them. They looked at me as if to say, "Who are you? What is going on?" I reminded them that I wanted this deal to work out for both of us and would be most grateful if they could find something that might not be good for me. They did not do it, not right away anyway, but I really wanted to do this thing right. I was pumped, and so I never backed down. By the end, they also identified some provisions that would be better for our side.

The project ended up doing very, very well. These two developers who were on the brink of bankruptcy came out very well, and so did we. They told me later that the approach to the negotiation also changed them, and that they decided that they want to do business like that in the future. We developed a lifelong relationship.

Does this mean it always works out well financially? I used to think that, but I realize now that it does not. We recently had a deal where acting legally we could have done some things to allow us to do very well on a real estate deal in these very troubled times. We chose to take a more transparent path, and it cost us a lot of money.

I asked him if people ever exploited him because of this openness. Jack answered:

In my view, the vast majority of the business people that I deal with are honorable. They will reflect back what you show to them. If you act honorably to them they will act honorably to you. If you get the relationship going down the right path, where you are actively looking out for them, they will in fact actively look out for you. It may not happen right away, but it will happen. If you are in a contentious situation and are always trying to outsmart the other guy, it is not healthy.

There are some people you can't work with. When you do what I have described, they think you are stupid or naive, and they seek to exploit it. You have to have your eyes open and be prepared to walk away from some deals.[3]

We mentioned in the last chapter that sometimes you have to not work with one customer for the sake of others. When Jack walked away from a deal, he did just that.

Don Flow, another modern-day leader, provides our second illustration of what transparency looks like in business. Don is the owner of thirty-two auto dealerships in North Carolina. Like Jack vanHartesvelt, Don is a business leader who decided he wanted to get more transparency into his business. Here is how describes his approach:

The traditional model in the automobile business has at the center point a transaction where both parties try to maximize their own position. Thus the auto dealer sees the customer as an element of the profit-maximization model. What we try to do is to change that model and ask, "How are we serving the customer?" This is a completely different starting point. At most of our stores, there's no negotiation. The price is given right up front to the customer.

The whole approach to sales, service, and everything else starts with, "If we have a covenant relationship with this customer, if we are to treat them like a valued friend, what would every interaction look like?"

In trying to incorporate this idea into the details of the way they do business, Flow Automotive came up with many innovations. Here is one of them:

Traditionally, automobile sales are different from sales of other products. Most auto dealerships have "no return" policies. We asked ourselves why auto sales should be different, and decided they should not be. We decided that if a customer was not happy with their purchase they could bring it back.

He found, however, that he had to revise his return policy.

One day, a customer came into our dealership on a Friday and bought a new Chevrolet Corvette. On Monday he brought it into the dealership and said he was not satisfied with the car and wanted his money back. It turns out he had purchased the car, driven to Florida for the weekend, and now wanted to turn it in. We decided this was too obvious a hole in our policy. On the other hand, we wanted to continue to strive for openness in all of our dealings. So we revised the policy to allow anyone to bring a car back and exchange it for one of equal or greater value. Sure, some people will exploit what you do, but we still wanted to err on the side of openness.[4]

Jim Sinegal, now retired, was CEO of Costco, the large, publicly traded international retail chain. In his career, Jim also chose to err on the side of transparency.

Costco is distinctive among its competitors for its policy of never marking anything up more than 14 percent (with an average mark-up of only 10 percent). Jim lowered prices on items when the wholesale price went down—even if market competition and customer awareness didn't require it. Costco also determined to make sure its employee wages and benefits led the industry. *Businessweek* reported that a Costco cashier with four years' experience could earn more than $40,000 with full benefits. We asked Jim how he decided to run the business this way:

> Part of it is just sound business thinking. . . . We operate this way because we believe philosophically that this is what we should be doing—but we also do it because of the nature of our business. People would always ask "What's the catch?" We wanted to make it clear that there were no catches.[5]

Jack vanHartesvelt, Don Flow, and Jim Sinegal went further toward transparency than many people do in business. All three recognized, however, that there were some people who were not trustworthy, some who would try to exploit them, and some who would push back in the name of profit. Having a clear picture of where you want to go and what kind of company you want to be helps you hold your ground, even in the face of opposition or others trying to exploit you. Joseph, in spite of his apparent trickery, seemed to have this goal as well. When he arrived at a point where he could trust his brothers, the transparency became fully evident.

How do we know where to draw these lines? Although most people would like a simple formula, I am convinced it is not that simple. I appreciate what Albert Einstein said: "You should make things as simple as possible, but no simpler." Generally, I would say that we should start with the truth and aim for transparency in all that we say and do. In some situations, despite truly acting with integrity, we may have to be slightly less transparent. Earlier in the chapter we recognized that there may be a case where we would be dishonest to save a life, recognizing this hierarchy of values. But as Yung pointed out, "This does not mean that lying is right in and of itself."

Bribery represents the ultimate lack of transparency, because it involves an "under the table payment" with no receipt. A friend of mine who works in Africa has committed to avoid paying a bribe and draws on the words of 1 John 1:7, "We walk in the light, as he is in the light." Moving transactions from the dark to the light is his way of putting more transparency in his business.

In addition to our personal relationships with God, most of us have the opportunity to connect with others, to bring in others' counsel to keep us from rationalizing or deluding ourselves into making a wrong decision. I asked Sherron Watkins, the whistle-blower from Enron whom we met in chapter 6, what she would do differently if she were to be faced with another situation like the one she confronted there. She answered, "If someone is in the unfortunate position where I was, I say don't go it alone. I should have found a few more people to go with me because then they could not have dismissed me as one lone person. And I would have been clearer in how to act."[6] Joseph didn't seem to have the opportunity for godly counsel with colleagues, but we generally do and should take advantage of it.

Joseph's use of trickery was not for personal or business gain; it was to see if a very special customer was trustworthy. Emulating him in a modern setting might land a business leader in court. But the concept of testing a customer for trustworthiness, done carefully, remains an important concept in business.

20

FEAR AND FORGIVENESS

In his role as CEO of the Egyptian International Food Company, Joseph had to deal with fear from two quite different sources—both of which parallel the two most common sources of fear in today's workplace. He dealt with his brothers, who feared him because of his position and power after he revealed himself to them. And he dealt with the Egyptians who feared external circumstances—the threat of starvation—when they ran out of money. We can draw insight for twenty-first-century business from the way he dealt with both kinds of fear in the people around him.

When Joseph revealed himself to his brothers, we see a vivid picture of fear: "Joseph said to his brothers, 'I am Joseph! Is my father still living?' But his brothers were not able to answer him, because they were terrified at his presence" (Genesis 45:3). We can practically feel their distress in this moment. They were fearful because they had done wrong—deliberate wrong. It was not an accident. But Joseph was able to put the situation into a bigger context, and he did what he could to quiet their terror: "Do not be distressed and do not be angry with yourselves for selling me here, because it was to save lives that God sent me ahead of you" (45:5).

Joseph looked to the big picture. He saw that although his brothers had done him wrong, this had led to the events that were now unfolding that would save the world from starvation. Understanding the issue in this bigger context changed the way Joseph saw the situation. Forgiveness and this type of fear represent two sides of the same coin. It should not be news to us that people, whether workers or the top boss, are imperfect. This imperfection shows up in small or big, willful issues. What Joseph's brothers had done to him clearly fit in the latter category.

Fear needs to be dealt with in the workplace because it is a deadly force. According to Peter Drucker, a management thought leader, fear of communicating openly and candidly is the silent killer of organizational performance. In *Shaping the Management Mind*, he argues that fear generates hostility toward innovation, produces resistance to change, and is incompatible with knowledge work.[1]

The way Joseph dealt with his brothers' fear is also a model for us today to look at the situation in a bigger context. As Soichiro Honda, the founder of Honda Motor Corporation, said, "Success is 99 percent failure."[2] Since no one is perfect, and there will be mistakes, dealing with errors constructively is the key to finding the bigger context and allowing an organization to learn from its mistakes—and establishing an environment of forgiveness allows this to happen.

A colleague of mine had recently taken a position with a large Internet retailer when someone in the IT department incorrectly updated the online pricing database. This took down the service in December, the biggest sales month of the year for this business. He expected a lot of yelling and finger-pointing, but was surprised with the response. After getting the system back online, a meeting was called to figure out what had happened. The person doing the update said he had made a mistake and it was his fault. But one of the other colleagues stepped forward to say that he had created the update procedure, and he recognized that the instructions were too easily misunderstood. Together they created a change to clarify the procedure.

The next day, they were called into the big boss's office to explain what had happened. Again, my colleague expected yelling and finger-pointing. The boss asked for an explanation, and the same person said what he had done. The second person again identified his role in the ambiguous procedure, and together they showed what they had done to fix it. The boss said, "Great. Let's get on with our work," and the meeting was over. No one was fired and no one yelled.

This illustrates how important it is to set the environment of the workplace so that problems can be solved and the process made better. An environment of fear leads only to problems being covered up, as we will see in the next example.

"We heard a loud bang, and the oxygen masks dropped down, and I knew at that point that something was wrong," said Damon Zwyker, a passenger on Alaska Airlines flight 536 en route from Seattle to Burbank on Tuesday, December 27, 2005. "It was absolutely the scariest thing I've ever had to go through in my entire life. I felt like I was lucky to be alive," added passenger Leslie Comstock.[3] Fortunately, the airplane was able to return safely to the Seattle airport after a foot-long hole blew in the fuselage of the airplane, causing the cabin to depressurize. Why did this happen?

Six months earlier, Alaska Airlines had laid off five hundred baggage workers at the Seattle airport in a labor dispute and subcontracted the work to a low-priced bidder. A ramp worker later acknowledged that he failed to immediately report striking the plane with a baggage cart, or baggage-belt machine, at the gate on Monday, December 26—the day before the incident. The worker told the agency that although the vehicle touched the plane, he was not aware he had dented it. The worker was suspended.

While this potentially serious incident worked out well, it proved to be a scary situation for the plane's passengers. Perhaps the worker was careless, or perhaps he was not well trained. In either case, recognizing the difficult labor situation, he was not willing to come forward to assure that he had not done serious damage, likely out of fear. When I met with Alaska Airlines CEO Brad Tilden, I asked him about this difficult period. He told me:

> If you look at the history of the company, there have been a couple of periods in the last 20, 30 years where relationships got pretty ragged, but we got through them. If you go back to 2005, Alaska had very high costs and we knew they needed to come down. We were trying to compete against JetBlue and Virgin and Frontier on many of our routes. Every one of our legacy airline competitors went through bankruptcy. Their costs came down, they shed pensions, they restructured and outsourced, and retired old airplanes that they didn't want to fly. We didn't go through bankruptcy, but to compete, our costs needed to come down.
>
> We had a binding-arbitration provision in our pilot contract, and we ultimately went to arbitration. Both sides presented their cases and we got new, significantly lower wage rates with our pilots. Pensions weren't changed at all. There were a couple of other changes to the contract, and our costs came down.
>
> In retrospect, I don't think we did a good job helping people understand what was happening in our industry, and what had to happen at Alaska for us to be able to compete successfully. These shortcomings made getting through some of our labor issues more difficult than it needed to be.[4]

According to a 2010 study by the Ethics Research Center, fear of retaliation for speaking up about ethical violations in the workplace not only affects whether workers are willing to report wrongdoing to management, but it also drives the level of misconduct itself.

Here is how another business leader dealt with fear in his workplace. In September 2006, Alan Mulally became CEO of Ford Motor Company. When he arrived, Ford was not a place where open communication took place: "The Ford culture had been so different. When they went to a meeting, they would have this huge book with all the answers. The bosses would ask questions and keep drilling until the presenter was humiliated and had to give up." Clearly, this is not a way to bring issues out into the open!

So Alan instituted a different type of review that encouraged openness, though it took a while to take hold. In the first three or four reviews with his staff, they reported the status of every project as "green," going well and on target! Finally he stopped one of the reviews and said, "You guys, in the last year we lost $14.7 billion. Is there anything that is not going well?" It was one of those defining moments. People were simply used to hiding the real situation.

The following week, Mark Fields, the executive in charge of launching the new Edge vehicle, reported his status as "red"— there was an issue with the hydraulic lift gate on the back. The room became deathly quiet. Everyone was wondering what was going to happen now: Would Mark be back next week? What was the price for a "red"? In another defining moment for Ford, what was Mulally's reaction?

> I start clapping. They were all looking at me. I said to Mark, "That is fabulous visibility. Are there any of us here that can help you, is there anything you need?" Immediately, purchasing and manufacturing engineering stepped up to help. By the next week we were ready to launch the vehicle.

An interesting footnote to this story is that in July 2014 when Alan retired, Mark Fields was named the new CEO of Ford. There is no guarantee of success when speaking up in this way. Although this was not Mark's only strength, his courage was indeed rewarded. Mulally gives this advice:

> You must make it safe to talk the truth. It is not about acting all "warm and fuzzy," but you have to know everything to make good decisions, and to get there you have got to make it safe when something goes wrong. If you yell at somebody when they put a yellow up, it is going to be green next week. They are human beings.[5]

Alan Mulally adds an important qualifier to the importance of forgiveness that we also see in the Joseph account. In both cases, it was of paramount importance to find out the truth, and you don't get there by shooting the messenger.

There may be limitations to forgiveness, however, or there may be situations where forgiveness is accompanied by natural consequences. A nurse who repeatedly gave the wrong medication may be forgiven but still fired. An accountant who stole from the company may be forgiven as a person but still fired. In a similar way, we saw Joseph testing his brothers before forgiving them. A leader needs wisdom, not formulas, for knowing and acting on these distinctions.

Alan Mulally and Joseph had the same responsibility. They needed to take the lead in creating an environment free of fear, and they needed to set the climate by initiating the offer of forgiveness. These leaders were able to step back and see the bigger picture. It would be great if no one, including the boss, ever failed or ever took a step that would disrupt their world. But that is not living in reality. Strong leaders create an environment where they can understand what is going on and deal with it, rather than cover it up. Although I have never found "forgiveness" on the value statement of a company—and I have looked at many such statements—doing this right is absolutely essential in any organization.

It would seem that this should end the matter, but in Joseph's story, as in our own lives, it is not that simple. Two other examples of fear in the workplace show up in his story. One is when the Egyptians run out of money and the famine is not yet over (we look at this situation in chapter 25). The second comes with Joseph's brothers after their father dies.

Joseph had called for the whole family of Jacob to come and live nearby, enjoying access to food during the famine period. But after the famine ended, Jacob died in Egypt and a new fear arose among Joseph's brothers:

> When Joseph's brothers saw that their father was dead, they said, "What if Joseph holds a grudge against us and pays us back for all the wrongs we did to him?" So they sent word to Joseph, saying, "Your father left these instructions before he died: 'This is what you are to say to Joseph: I ask you to forgive your brothers the sins and the wrongs they committed in treating you so badly.' Now please forgive the sins of the servants of the God of your father." When their message came to him, Joseph wept. His brothers then came and threw themselves down before him. "We are your slaves," they said. (Genesis 50:15–18)

Had Joseph's brothers truly believed his offer of forgiveness, or did they assume it was conditional on the life of their father? They were not ready to trust the forgiveness they had been granted. They felt guilty—and they were. But Joseph had forgiven them, not for their father but for God. He went on to say, "'So then, don't be afraid. I will provide for you and your children.' And he reassured them and spoke kindly to them" (50:21).

We shouldn't be surprised if offering forgiveness takes a while to "stick," and our own motivations are misconstrued. We wrote earlier about "theory of mind," the ability to see a situation through the eyes of another, something most of us are not very good at. The brothers had seen the situation only through their own eyes. And when forgiveness is offered in the workplace, we should not be surprised if the receiver assumes false motives. It may require another conversation. We saw this also in the situation at Ford. After he had commended the person who stepped forward and identified a problem, Alan Mulally said that in the next week's review people actually watched to see if the person really returned, or if he had been fired after the acknowledgment. It takes time to drive fear out of the workplace.

Perhaps this is part of what Jesus meant when he answered a question from Peter about how many times he should forgive his brother: "Not seven times, but seventy-seven times" (Matthew 18:22).

I remember a time in the early 1990s at Boeing when we were going through significant cutbacks and people were fearful for their jobs. One day I called a voluntary meeting of everyone in the organization over lunchtime and said I would share as openly as I could about what was going on in the company. I made it clear that no question was out of bounds and that I would answer with as much knowledge as I had. Almost half of the organization showed up in the theater where we gathered. We continued these meetings weekly through the crisis, and I learned an important lesson during that period. People's imagined fears are often greater than reality. Clear and open communication is vital to alleviate this kind of fear. It must be honest. You can't sugarcoat difficult news.

This is the kind of open communication that Joseph established, and it was vital to reducing fear. In this next chapter, we will see how this open communication is demonstrated in another difficult situation.

21

FAIRNESS AND JUSTICE

We saw in chapter 17, "Executing the Strategy," that a strategy must be adapted to unforeseen situations as the work moves forward. One situation that was not spelled out in Joseph's plan was what to do if the Egyptian people ran out of money to pay for the food. This was the problem that he now encountered.

> When the money of the people of Egypt and Canaan was gone, all of Egypt came to Joseph and said, "Give us food. Why should we die before your eyes? Our money is all gone."
> "Then bring your livestock," said Joseph. So . . . he gave them food in exchange for their horses, their sheep and goats, their cattle and donkeys. And he brought them through that year with food in exchange for all their livestock. (Genesis 47:15–17)

While this adaptation to the strategy sustained them through the year, the famine continued and the Egyptians were back in the same situation a year later.

> They came to him the following year and said, "We cannot hide from our lord the fact that since our money is gone and our livestock belongs to you, there is nothing left for our lord except our bodies and our land. Why should we perish before your eyes— we and our land as well? Buy us and our land in exchange for food, and we with our land will be in bondage to Pharaoh. Give us seed so that we may live and not die, and that the land may not become desolate."

So Joseph bought all the land of Egypt for Pharaoh. . . .
Joseph reduced the people to servitude. (Genesis 47:18–20, 21)

We see an interesting contrast between the first time the people ran out of money and the second. In the first instance, they asked to be given food, but Joseph demanded payment and took it in their livestock. The second time they must have known Joseph would not simply give them food. So they proposed giving up their land and becoming slaves, and Joseph accepted their offer. But Joseph offered more than they had asked for.

> "Now that I have bought you and your land today for Pharaoh, here is seed for you so you can plant the ground. But when the crop comes in, give a fifth of it to Pharaoh. The other four-fifths you may keep as a seed for the fields and as food for yourselves and your households and your children." (Genesis 47:23–24)

For the twenty-first-century reader, this may seem like harsh treatment. We shudder at the use of the word *slavery*. This version of slavery, however, is unlike our modern use of the term. Joseph gave them a way out by enabling them to keep 80 percent of their income to work their way back to freedom. The response of the people suggests that they saw it this way. " 'You have saved our lives,' they said. 'May we find favor in the eyes of our lord; we will be in bondage to Pharaoh' " (Genesis 47:25).

As an aside, we gain a glimpse into the management style of Joseph here. That he had these conversations at all is a tribute to his level of openness and engagement. Remember, Joseph did not have to meet anyone halfway. Pharaoh had said that no one would lift a hand or foot in all of Egypt without Joseph's approval. He had even said that people would go before Joseph calling out, "Make way!" So it was Joseph's choice to have what these days we might call an open door policy.

Those who do not work in a large organization may assume that this is the norm, but it is not. For example, I was doing an ethics seminar for a regional bank in the Northwest. The CEO

asked me to have lunch with the people who reported directly
to him, just to gain insight into how they saw ethics and their
work. To my surprise, the conversation opened a flood of concern regarding the CEO, who rarely communicated with them.
When I shared this general impression with the CEO at the end
of the day, he explained that this was part of his management
style. His father had told him never to get to close to people who
worked for him, because one day he might have to fire one of
them and it would cloud his judgment. This stands high up on
my list of bad management practices and certainly undermined
the productivity of his team.

By contrast, when Jim Sinegal was CEO of Costco, he answered his own telephone, walked down the stairs personally to
take me back to his office for our interview, and wore a Costco
badge with the name "Jim." No title, no special markings. He
talked with anyone.

How should we think about Joseph's decision? My more
conservative friends would likely side with Joseph on this issue,
though they may say he was being too generous. After all, the
Egyptians hadn't provided for themselves and that was their
problem. My more liberal friends would take the other side. They
would argue that Joseph had acquired the grain from them in
the first place, and he owed it to them. It was not right for his
company, and through his company the government, to profit
from their plight. Certainly this interpretation would focus on
the evils of slavery.

There is a strong parallel between what happened in Egypt
and what happened in the United States during the mortgage crisis and subsequent economic meltdown. And there is an equally
strong parallel between the way people on either side of our political divide would have responded to Joseph's decisions and the
way they did respond to the mortgage crisis. I see in the economic
part of Joseph's solution, however, something more innovative
and helpful than I have seen in the recent mortgage crisis.

In Joseph's time, people had run out of money and couldn't afford to buy food, facing starvation. In the modern crisis, people ran out of money and couldn't afford the payments on their homes, facing eviction. The deal that Joseph offered was that people would lose ownership of their land but could stay there to earn their living. But now they would pay 20 percent of what they earned as a tax to the government. A modern translation of this solution would have the homes belonging to the bank, but the people being allowed to stay in their homes, paying rent of 20 percent of their income.

Granted, the modern problem is much more complicated than the problem Joseph faced. In the modern economic crisis, some people lost their jobs while seeing the value on their home drop and the payments increase (due to a complex mortgage instrument). These people could be helped with the kind of solution Joseph proposed. Others in the modern crisis were hurt because they "bought" six homes hoping to profit from rising home prices. Or some bought much more expensive homes than they could afford.

There were lots of challenges for Joseph in implementing his solution. The Egyptian International Food Company would now have to be in the land management business and the livestock management business, something it was not designed to do. Similarly, banks are not set up to be property managers. But it was an innovative solution that meant, in Joseph's time, people faced natural consequences for running out of money but still had a way out. It would be tough for both sides through the rest of the famine where 20 percent of the income would be meager for both. In the years beyond the famine, however, there was hope for both sides.

In Egypt's case, I see problems with siding with the liberal view on the economic issue, arguing that Joseph should have simply given them the food. After all, why did the people run out of grain and money, and what was their responsibility in that outcome? During the seven years of plenty, they were being taxed 20 percent. They watched as huge granaries were raised in their own back yards. What did they do with the 80 percent of the crop they kept for themselves? What responsibility did they have for setting some of this aside for themselves and their families? It would be easy to argue that they didn't know the famine was coming. But why was Joseph collecting the grain? Why did they need to raise their standard of living to the level they did with the bountiful harvest?

In all likelihood, people in Egypt did what people in the United States did on the boom side of the housing market. They assumed that the growth would last forever, and rather than putting something aside, they simply escalated their standard of living. They upgraded their chariots, bought a second or third home, and continued living on the edge. This is the way it was in the mid-2000s among real estate agents and many others.

According to Bev Bothel, a managing partner at Windemere Real Estate in Bellevue, Washington, here's what it looked like:

> This was the ultimate boom market. Builders were building lots of products. There was a lot of demand. The day-to-day real estate that took place included multiple offers on homes and often a feeding frenzy of pricing.
>
> As the frenzy built, lots of people saw gold in this market and hopped on board. Some people came on part time to sell real estate, and they did not understand this is a full-time task requiring full-time thought processes and a long-term view.
>
> Agents are in the same position as buyers and sellers. Everyone has a level at which they live. In the last five years, real estate brokers have had a very comfortable level. But when you don't sell a house, you don't get paid. So this is a very difficult time.[1]

During this very difficult time, some former real estate agents went into bankruptcy, and some took their own lives. Difficult indeed.

The conservative element of Pharaoh's advisors might have urged Joseph to take the people's homes and their land. Let the neighbors feed those who couldn't feed themselves. Too bad the people weren't more responsible. The liberal group of advisors might have urged Joseph to give the people the food they needed. Joseph, however, did neither, but found an innovative economic solution that likely satisfied neither side, but focused on natural consequences along with compassion and fairness.

Independent of the economic crisis, we face a similar challenge in dealing with poverty in the world today. Here the debate is between aid and economic development. Long-term aid creates dependence, while economic development done well creates a sustainable future. Today, as in Joseph's time, however, these are not hard and fast boundaries. I am sure there were some then, as there are now, who are unable to work, and in some cases aid is the only solution.

My friend Tim Weinhold recently argued for another biblical model that tries to find the path between aid and economic development. In the book of Ruth, the wealthy are instructed not to harvest their fields to the boundary, but to leave some of the harvest for the poor. It is not packaged and delivered to them, but they could come into the fields and harvest it themselves, a kind of transition model between dependency and sustainability. Joseph's model offers something similar. Nevertheless, reducing people to servitude has consequences, and these do indeed show up later.

22

TEMPTATION OF POWER

A s we saw in chapter 5, Joseph responded honorably to sexual temptation. And as we saw in chapter 15, he prepared himself for dealing with the temptations of his position. But the lure of temptation can be relentless over a long period of time, and we get some glimpses of how he dealt with two other major temptations—power and money—later in the story. We will consider his dealings with power in this chapter and with money in the next.

When Pharaoh appointed Joseph to his position, he gave him power and authority that few could handle well. "Pharaoh said to Joseph, 'I hereby put you in charge of the whole land of Egypt. . . . I am Pharaoh, but without your word no one will lift a hand or foot in all of Egypt'" (Genesis 41:41, 44).

We saw in chapter 15 that Joseph took his work seriously, recognizing the importance and the enormity of the task, that he held firm to his relationship with his God, and that he had an Egyptian family to keep bringing him back to reality. So he had some safeguards to protect him from allowing this much power to go to his head. But as Lord Acton famously said: "Power tends to corrupt, and absolute power corrupts absolutely. Great men are almost always bad men."

There are two ways that a person in authority can abuse power. One concerns how they deal with those to whom they are accountable. Are they thinking they are bigger than their boss, competing for the boss's position, or trying to establish how much they can get away with? The second concerns how they deal with the people who are under their authority. Do they listen to their subordinates' insights? Do they engage them in decision-making? Or do they use their position of power to make all of the decisions by themselves?

Joseph made some remarkable and instructive choices when it came to how he interacted with Pharaoh. There are many parts of the story that illustrate this, but here are two in particular. After Joseph had made himself known to his brothers and forgiven them, it was time to reconnect with his father. He asked his brothers to let his father know that he was alive and to bring him to Egypt so he could see him again. Joseph had the power and authority from Pharaoh to make this decision on his own. He could have spent "company money" to bring them all to Egypt and have them stay there to wait out the famine. Instead, he engaged Pharaoh in this big decision. Pharaoh said,

> "Bring your father and your families back to me. I will give you the best of the land of Egypt, and you can enjoy the fat of the land.
> "You are also directed to tell them, 'Do this: Take some carts from Egypt for your children and your wives and get your father and come. Never mind about your belongings, because the best of all Egypt will be yours.'" (Genesis 45:18–20)

Pharaoh later instructed Joseph to put "those from his family of special ability" (Genesis 47:6) to be in charge of his own livestock. And Pharaoh directed them to live in the land of Goshen.

After living in Egypt for seventeen years, Jacob instructed Joseph that when he died he was not to be buried there, but that his body was to be taken back to Canaan. Again, when Jacob died, Joseph might have left without notice, or just told Pharaoh he was leaving, and gone back with his father's body to bury him. But he went to Pharaoh and said, "Now let me go up to bury my father and then I will return" (Genesis 50:5). Pharaoh not only agreed to let Joseph go, but he also said that he would have his officials accompany him, providing transportation and logistics support. "Chariots and horsemen also went up with him. It was a very large company" (50:9).

In both of these situations, Joseph had the power to make a decision but chose to engage his boss in the process. Why did he do this? Joseph probably understood something that it took me much longer to learn. I found out when I was managing the research organization at Boeing that one of my bosses did not like surprises. I remember coming back from a meeting with a senior executive on the manufacturing side of the company, someone whom my boss knew well. My boss phoned me as I was walking into my office, irate that I would meet with this person without telling him. In retrospect, I realized that he had a fragile relationship with this person and wanted to make sure that nothing undermined it. I should have engaged him when I set up the appointment.

Joseph did well to keep his boss informed on potentially sensitive matters. Some might say he was limiting his own power and authority by doing so. But taking care to limit one's authority is a good thing when done wisely. It keeps the power in check, and demonstrates respect for the leader.

From what we can read in the text, Joseph did less well in engaging those people who helped him in the distribution of the grain. In the situation we looked at before, when the Egyptians had run out of money and food, they came to him with a proposal: "Buy us and our land in exchange for food, and we with our land will be in bondage to Pharaoh." There is no indication that Joseph involved those working for him in deciding what to do. He simply went forward with this plan.

Wouldn't it have been helpful for Joseph to engage some of his Egyptian stewards in this decision, both to better understand the Egyptian way of thinking and to analyze the possible implications of this decision? He seemed to use his position of power and authority to simply make the decision by himself. Some would argue that he had God on his side, but this is dangerous territory. Humanly speaking, we can easily delude ourselves and it is good to engage counsel. Even if Joseph was able to get by with this, we should be careful about following him here.

Dennis Bakke, the CEO of the multinational energy company AES Corporation, concluded that it was important to "give up power" by allowing others to be involved in key decisions. Here is his story:

> In most organizations, the more important the decision, the more senior the decision maker is. That is, the people who get paid a lot or have their big titles are the ones who make the big decisions. This is true whether it's profit-making, a non-profit, or the government. Because of this practice, most people don't get to make important decisions . . . and the status quo of 85 to 90 percent of the people having miserable jobs would continue.
>
> We decided the decision maker should be the person closest to the action, or the one who has had the most experience in that particular area. And yes, there are problems with that. How do you avoid having lone rangers simply making decisions on their own that would affect many people? We didn't want that. We all know that we're individuals first, but we're also put in community. We needed to figure out how an organization can put these two things together.
>
> So we required the person leading the decision to get advice from others affected by the decision. In the case of a very large decision that would impact the company, the advice needed to include senior executives, and even the board of directors. A person could be fired for not getting advice. But the person did not have to be a senior officer, or have a long history with the company, in order to be able to make the decision, and having asked for advice, it was their decision to make.[1]

While this may sound risky, it engaged people who knew what was going on at the ground level, and Dennis found that better decisions were made. Some may be unwilling to go as far as he did in allowing people to make the decision, but there is precedent for this approach.

In the Garden of Eden, God gave Adam a number of tasks to do. One of Adam's first assignments was to name the animals. In the Bible, "naming" means more than putting a label on things: it is more like our concept of branding. I can picture Adam sitting on a hillside watching and studying each animal and then deciding on an appropriate name. "[God] brought them to the man to see what he would name them; and whatever the man called each living creature, that was its name" (Genesis 2:19). Many modern-day leaders would say, "Let me know what you think, and I will decide whether or not I approve."

Another powerful leader explained to me how he dealt with the power in his position. I asked General Peter Pace, former chair of the Joint Chiefs of Staff—the top person in the U.S. military—how a general could make a "top-down" decision in the rigid command and control structure of the military. Here is his response:

> I think your premise is wrong. In the military, the highest level strategy comes top down, as it does in most businesses. But once a direction is identified, leadership to carry out this strategy is top down, bottom up, and sideways. Once the chain of command issues an order of intent, the folks at the lower levels use their own initiative and leadership in carrying this out. I think leadership "up" is at least as important as leadership "down" in the military.
>
> I like to listen as much as I can. When I come into a new organization, I spend as much time as I can just talking to folks about what's going right and what's going wrong. Inside the military, there is always a senior enlisted person who you can talk with to find out their perspective and get their guidance on whatever is happening. I gather senior leaders' perspectives. Then I can put together my own thoughts of what I heard and make decisions. When we get together I tell people what I understand,

where we're going to go, and how we can get there. But I always use examples of who told me what so that they know that I have been listening and paying attention. Those on the ground know a lot more about the details of what is going on than any senior officer, and I would be a fool not to gain from this knowledge.[2]

General Pace's willingness to learn from those under his authority was a strength, not a weakness. Like Alan Mulally, Dennis Bakke, and other effective leaders we have met, the general was made stronger by his willingness to learn from others in his organization.

Joseph did some good things by holding his power in check, both by not seeking after personal gain and in his relationship with Pharaoh. We can learn a great deal from him here. We do not see evidence that he engaged the people under his authority in his decisions. I would see this as a weakness in his leadership.

23

TEMPTATION OF MONEY

One challenge an executive faces in dealing with money comes from the temptation to use the position to accumulate personal wealth. Convicted executives from Tyco, Enron, and other modern companies that went drastically wrong fell into this trap. Disgraced bankers from the recent worldwide economic collapse also failed in this way. We have already discussed some of Joseph's encounters with money and wealth, but by considering them together here we can get the big picture:

1. Joseph's first encounter with money came when he was sold into slavery for twenty shekels of silver (37:43).

2. The second was when, as Potiphar's head slave, he was entrusted with everything Potiphar owned (39:8).

3. After Pharaoh promoted him, he was given a huge compensation package (41:42–43). Though we are not told the amount of his compensation, he was given responsibility for all of Pharaoh's wealth.

4. When he was collecting grain, he stopped counting it "because it was beyond measure" (41:49).

5. When his brothers came for food, "Joseph gave orders to fill their bags with grain and to put each man's silver in the mouth of his sack" (42:23).

6. He repeated this process after the brothers' second trip for food (44:1).

7. When the brothers returned from Egypt to get their father, "To each of them he gave new clothing, but to Benjamin he gave three hundred shekels of silver and five sets of clothes" (45:22).

8. During the famine, "Joseph collected all the money that was to be found in Egypt and Canaan in payment for the grain they were buying, and he brought it to Pharaoh's palace" (47:14).

9. When the people ran out of money and he collected their land for food, "Joseph bought all the land of Egypt for Pharaoh" (47:20).

10. When he taxed the people's earnings near the end of the famine, he commanded them to "give a fifth to Pharaoh" (47:24).

The remarkable thing about Joseph and his interaction with money is a complete lack of focus on money for personal gain. Whether he was managing wealth for Potiphar or for Pharaoh, his focus seemed to be directed toward his responsibility to them, not what he could achieve for himself. In this, Joseph stands in stark contrast to both ancient and modern leaders.

The Apostle Paul said, "For the love of money is the root of all kinds of evil" (1 Timothy 6:10). The writer of the book of Ecclesiastes said, "Whoever loves money never has money enough; whoever loves wealth is never satisfied with his income. This too is meaningless" (5:10).

Some may think that because Joseph had a generous compensation package, he didn't have a need for more. But that has not been the case for modern leaders. Guy Kawasaki, venture capitalist and former Apple executive, remarked:

There is something about power and money that just corrupts people. What would cause an executive who makes $15–$20 million per year to pad his expense report for a few thousand? These emperors are truly naked, but they believe they are clothed.[1]

Jeff Van Duzer, dean of the School of Business and Economics at Seattle Pacific University, writes,

> One might guess that with larger and larger fortunes, the marginal utility of each next dollar would decrease. In fact, my experience is that the desire for enhanced accumulations tends to be stronger among the wealthier.[2]

While the problem of "always wanting more" is especially a problem for the wealthy, at some level it is a problem for everyone. Those making a lot less money can suffer from being envious, or they can rationalize that they don't have a problem because they have far fewer "things" than those on top. It's a challenge to learn to be content regardless of where we are on the economic scale.

Abuse can happen at all levels. I drove my car to the airport for my first business trip, and two colleagues asked me to pick them up. When I filled in my expense report I turned in mileage for driving plus the parking charge. I was surprised to see that the colleagues I had picked up both turned in cab fare to and from the airport on their expense reports. I was too surprised to know how to react.

It is interesting that Joseph stopped counting the grain collected during good times. The reason given is that it was "beyond measure," but that has not stopped the wealthiest of our society from measuring their worth as a way to keep score. Athletes and celebrities of our day also use the size of their contracts as a way to measure respect. I think he stopped counting because he believed there would be enough grain and the exact amount was not needed to feed his ego.

In addition to the greed that money seems to foster, money affects us in other ways. Daniel Kahneman, social scientist and

Nobel Prize winner in economics, showed through many experiments that focusing on money drives us toward selfishness, isolation, and short-term thinking.[3] Steve Reinemund, former chairman and CEO of PepsiCo and dean of Business at Wake Forest University, says:

> Faith, unfortunately, doesn't isolate you from making bad judgments or even making mistakes of greed. But hopefully it broadens the horizons from which decisions are made. It is hard to justify in my mind that one would define success solely as earnings per share (EPS) growth on a short-term basis; there are so many other important constituencies. The EPS measure alone just fails for a business.[4]

Short-term thinking and money have dominated our own culture. It is vital to keep the long term in view and not give in to simply meeting short-term targets. Don Flow, the owner and CEO of Flow Automotive whom we met earlier, developed practices to help his business move away from focusing on short-term gain. Here is the way he described several of their approaches:

> We have a number of unconditional service commitments. The first is, if we do not repair your vehicle correctly the first time, you don't pay for additional repair. If it's not right, we come and pick up your car, we repair it no matter what the cost is to us, and return it to you. We believe we're supposed to be professional and you're paying us to diagnose it correctly, so we don't think we have the right to charge you again for something we charged you for the first time. Second, we make a commitment to complete the repair at the time promised. So if we say it's going to be ready at 2:30, and it's not, we'll take a car to your home or office and bring your car back to you when it is finished so you're not inconvenienced. Thirdly, when we give an estimate, that's the only price it'll ever be. If we misdiagnosed and found out that it wasn't a $100 repair but it was a $500 repair, we eat the difference.
>
> We did a study and found that the people who typically paid the least for the cars were the most able to pay. Those least able to pay paid the most. For me, it was wrong to take advantage

of the least able, a clear violation of the biblical mandate in the book of Proverbs.

So we have a customer-centric selling process. You don't have to be a tough negotiator, or more educated, to get a fair price. If you've got a Ph.D. or if you're a janitor, you'll pay the same price for the vehicle.[5]

I asked Don if he could make money operating his business in this way. He said that these practices fostered the customers' trust, which created value in the long term although it could cost his business in the short term.

Perhaps this was part of Joseph's protection against the allure of money as well. His project lasted fourteen years. At no point would he be able to shorten his horizons of thinking. From the first bundles of grain collected during the good times to the last distributed during the famine, it was always necessary to keep the long-term picture in view. Taking his eye off the objective during the collection phase might mean failure to collect enough grain to last through the famine. Short-term focus in the distribution phase might mean running out of food, so Joseph had to be long-term oriented.

Jeff Van Duzer offers another antidote to allowing money to control you: "I find that the act of giving (rather than the amount of giving) is most helpful. Whenever I give money away, I am, in effect, declaring that money does not define my intrinsic worth."[6] I wonder if Joseph, in giving the money back to his brothers when they purchased grain, was doing this as well. In his act of giving the money back to his brothers, we should notice another protection Joseph created for himself around money. He engaged others in doing this, rather than trying to do it by himself. He instructed the steward to put the money in the bag. Because of the control money can have on us, lessening our vulnerability through creating accountability is a helpful guideline.

The one anomaly in Joseph's exemplary handling of money was when he gave the extra amount of money and clothing to

Benjamin for their return trip to get their father. Certainly this was not Joseph grasping at money for personal gain. But it was using money to perpetuate the same problem that Jacob had created for Joseph. Joseph was using wealth to demonstrate favoritism. Hadn't this kind of grief already caused enough problems for the family? Why did he perpetuate it? And was this related to the little barb he threw in at the end when he sent them back to Jacob? "Don't quarrel on the way!" he told his brothers (Genesis 45:24). Maybe this detail is here to demonstrate that our heroes are not perfect, and the pain of his brothers' mistreatment still rankled him at some level. It took a while before Joseph's brothers really accepted his offer of forgiveness. And perhaps it took a while for Joseph to fully accept it himself. Sometimes we ourselves struggle with the issue of forgiveness, repeating patterns from our past.

Despite this one incident, Joseph demonstrated a remarkable commitment to avoid becoming a slave to money. He may have been affected by his early education with his father, who had focused a great deal of his life on accumulating wealth for himself. Maybe he was shaped by being sold for money by his brothers, an experience that must have been demeaning at best. Or perhaps the preparation discussed in chapter 15 allowed him to avoid getting caught up in personal greed.

24

GLOBALIZATION

In today's language, the Egyptian International Food Company might be called a multinational global corporation. As we trace back through the story of Joseph, we will see precursors to many of the challenges and opportunities that confront twenty-first-century multinational corporations. Early in the story, when Joseph has just been captured by his brothers, we read,

> As they sat down to eat their meal they looked up and saw a caravan of Ishmaelites coming from Gilead. Their camels were loaded with spices, balm, and myrrh, and they were on their way to take them down to Egypt. . . . So when the Midianite merchants came by, his brothers pulled Joseph up out of the cistern and sold him for twenty shekels of silver to the Ishmaelites, who took him to Egypt. (Genesis 37:25, 28)

Here is a picture of international trade, where the goods of one country are transported to another for sale. This part of globalization has been going on for centuries. But this passage raises another question. These merchants were apparently eager to expand their product base and were accountable to no one. Who controls the rules of what can and cannot be sold? In this case, they might have added the slave trade to their business in spices, balm, and myrrh on the spot. Where is the accountability?

The problem of accountability is equally troubling in modern globalized business. The early foundations for modern capitalism are often attributed to Adam Smith's classic book *The Wealth of Nations*. An oft-quoted line from that book is: "It is not from the benevolence of the butcher, the brewer or the baker, that we expect our dinner, but from their regard to their own interest."

Smith is making the case that individuals acting in their own self-interest will together address the common good. But when Adam Smith wrote this in 1776, he was referring to a butcher, a baker, and a brewer who lived in the same town, whom you would meet on the street. If something was wrong with the bread, or if the butcher had introduced a new lower-quality cut of meat, you could talk with him about it the next day. They had a natural accountability to their customers and their community that gets lost in the global world of commerce. That challenge existed for international traders in Joseph's time, and it is even more common today. If the small-town brewer started engaging in illegal business practices, he would be called out on it in the community. Who can call out the faceless multinational corporation?

The next picture of global business in Joseph's story comes when Pharaoh appoints Joseph to head the Egyptian International Food Company. It is one thing to have international trade, but a much rarer thing, until recently, to draw on international talent, particularly at the top levels of a company. In 2003, I talked with Prabhu Guptara, who at the time was the executive director of organizational development for the Wolfsberg Executive Development Center of UBS (initially United Bank of Switzerland). Guptara himself demonstrates today's international flavor of business. He was born in India, is a British citizen, and in 2003 he was working at UBS in Switzerland. Here is what he said about leadership at UBS:

> Only fifteen years ago, UBS was a very Swiss bank. And through a series of mergers and acquisitions it gradually became more and more European, and then finally more and more international. For example, our incoming chief financial officer for the whole group is Australian. We have had a chief executive who is British. Though it's still necessary in a Swiss bank to have a sufficient number of people on the board who can speak Swiss German,

which is the local dialect, it is not necessary for somebody who is chief financial officer to speak even a word of German, at least when he or she arrives on the scene.[1]

Joseph's promotion to a leadership role may have been surprising then, but it was truly a precursor to business in the twenty-first century.

Another event in the Joseph story mirrors today's globalization. "And all the world came to Egypt to buy grain from Joseph, because the famine was severe everywhere" (Genesis 41:57). There is an interdependency that is created through these global connections. In our modern world, Greg Page, CEO and chairman of Cargill, speaks to the positive side of this interdependency. Going against the popular argument for raising and eating food locally, he argues that our transportation infrastructure allows us to grow wheat in the area where rain and soil conditions allow the best wheat to be raised, to grow rice where that is best raised, and so forth, and then simply move the food to where it is needed. Some may be concerned about the cost of this transportation, either economically or ecologically, but he says,

> It is possible to move one ton of grain by ship over 2,000 miles with a single gallon of fuel. Thus the impact of a $100 per barrel rise in oil prices on the added cost to move a ton of wheat from Canada to Egypt would be less than $8 a ton. . . . You can see how the importance of capturing the comparative advantage of an area's water, soil and climate through free trade overwhelms the modest amount of energy needed to move food to areas of demand.[2]

Of course, those advocating local food creation and consumption offer a different argument. They may argue for taste and familiarity with growing practices. Further, interdependence can allow one nation to hold another hostage as Egypt had the opportunity to do when all nations depended on them for food. Perhaps oil is a modern-day picture of this.

Two more elements of global business become a part of the story when the brothers arrive in Egypt looking for food. Joseph said to them,

> "It is just as I told you. You are spies!" . . . And he put them all in custody for three days. . . . Reuben replied [to his brothers], "Didn't I tell you not to sin against the boy? Now we must give an accounting for his blood." They did not realize Joseph could understand them because he was using an interpreter. (Genesis 42:14, 17, 22–23)

First, we notice Joseph rather arbitrarily putting his brothers in prison. Today, his actions would likely have been considered inappropriate in most parts of the world, but unfortunately not all. This is not just a question of the law and which products can be sold, but how people from other countries can be dealt with under the law. This has an effect on global business today in many dimensions. Some countries have laws (or no laws at all) that allow for child labor, or for polluting the environment, or requiring a bribe. And yes, in some countries visiting businesspeople can be put in prison with little recourse. Knowing the laws in various countries and understanding the complexities of doing business under different legal systems is a part of today's environment of global business. For example, an American businessperson paying a bribe in a country where this is the favored practice can still be fined or imprisoned back in the United States under the Foreign Corrupt Practices Act. Again, the practices of the Egyptian International Food Company offer a small foretaste of the complexity of global business today.

Second, we observe that the brothers had difficulty communicating during this transaction due to the language barrier. Joseph spoke with them through an interpreter, and Reuben did not know that he could understand them. Although global transportation and trade are much easier today, this problem still applies. A young woman I know runs a business with manufacturing done in China, so she makes frequent trips there. They view her as the stereotypical "dumb blond" American, but she is a good businessperson and has learned Chinese. She gains considerable advantage in her negotiations because she can listen in on her business partners' strategy discussions. Joseph must have learned the Egyptian language while in prison, and as we heard Guptara say earlier, it is sometimes necessary for a newly recruited executive to learn another language as well.

Yet knowing the language, knowing the laws, attracting talent, and carrying out international trade are not enough for true globalization. As Guptara went on to say in our discussion:

> But I would argue that this [international talent] alone does not create a global mind-set. Because it could be the case that people coming from around the globe have to somehow fit into your national culture to be able to get into the top. The ability to be able to adapt to different cultures, go seamlessly to different parts of the world and absorb ideas is really the heart of being global. I wouldn't claim that we have reached our goal, but that's our journey.[3]

A small recognition of the need for a truly global attitude comes in Joseph's story as well. As Joseph was preparing his brothers to meet Pharaoh, he shared with them some of what he had learned about differences in customs between the two kingdoms:

> "When Pharaoh calls you in and asks, 'What is your occupation?' you should answer, 'Your servants have tended livestock from our boyhood on, just as our fathers did.' Then you will be allowed to settle in the region of Goshen, for all shepherds are detestable to the Egyptians." (Genesis 46:33–34)

Understanding different customs and tastes allowed Joseph's brothers to avoid an embarrassing *faux pas* and led to an employment opportunity as well. Today we see that it can create opportunity for new markets as well. Modern multinational companies have this understanding down to a science. Steve Reinemund, when he was chairman of PepsiCo, commented on the company's international product mix:

> We could not ship low-cost products very far because of the quality and the cost. So, all of our products were developed within the countries in which we sell them. We have very little export/import of finished goods. We do have some export/import of raw materials in some cases. Before we could sell potato chips in China, we had to spend several years developing the potato crop, because that's not an agricultural product that was well developed in China. We are vertically integrated in almost every country now. For the most part we develop, make and move, and sell our products within the boundaries of the countries.

> We try to have the basic product as close as possible to a worldwide standard. Where the difference would be is in the flavorings and the seasonings. For example, we have seasonings in China that we wouldn't have in other places. However, increasingly what we are finding, particularly as the United States becomes more diverse, [is that] products that are successfully sold in India, for instance, become popular in the United States as well.

> The key in a consumer products company is to have that balance of listening to the consumers and serving the consumers locally, but leveraging major technologies and learning to cross businesses whether it's best-practice sharing or technology standards. We found that balance is really important and our most effective leaders around the world are leaders who are good listeners, good innovators, and flexible, to be able to take these things back and forth.[4]

Coca-Cola vice president Bonnie Wurzbacher offers similar insight:

> Understanding local tastes and being able to sell and deliver those brands and packages in a way that meets local needs is why we have 3,000 packages. If you have ever gone to another country and found a Coca-Cola product in a tiny little can or in returnable glass, it's because they are meeting the local needs

and tastes and affordability measures of that market. That's why the local part is so important.[5]

The twenty-first century has just begun, but already it is being referred to as the century of global business. While that pace is clearly picking up in the modern era, we see that many of the roots of modern global business were already in place in this ancient story set in Egypt. Globalization is today, and was in Joseph's day, much more than international trade. Its practices are challenged by differing laws, customs, tastes, transportation, and talent issues, all of which were a part of the story in Egypt. The big difference in twenty-first-century globalization is technology, which introduces more than a quantitative change. Both outsourcing and automation, which are enabled by technology, affect jobs and opportunities for people around the world. Although Joseph's story is not an exact replica of a modern multinational business, we see in his story the precursor to many modern challenges for globalized business.

25

DID JOSEPH
ULTIMATELY FAIL?

Joseph did not have a very good plan. Look at the end of the
story. The net result was that the Egyptians were all slaves to the
Pharaoh because they had to sell their animals, their land, and
eventually themselves in order to keep from starving. And Jacob's family all ended up in Egypt where they ultimately became
slaves. How could you call this a good plan?

This is what a friend said to me when I told him I was writing this book. Indeed, my friend was right about the end
result. As we saw in chapter 20, as a result of Joseph's plan the
Egyptians were reduced to slavery. And while the Israelites (the
family of Jacob) were protected from the famine while in Goshen, the apparently favorable treatment they received during
the famine may have created a problem between them and the
Egyptians. The first part of the book of Exodus gives us, in my
friend's words, the "net result":

> Now Joseph and all his brothers and all that generation died,
> but the Israelites were fruitful and multiplied greatly and became
> exceedingly numerous, so that the land was filled with them.
> Then a new king, who did not know about Joseph, came to
> power in Egypt. "Look," he said to his people, "the Israelites have
> become much too numerous for us. Come, we must deal shrewdly
> with them or they will become even more numerous and, if war

breaks out, will join our enemies, fight against us and leave the country."

So they put slave masters over them to oppress them with forced labor, and they built Pithom and Rameses as store cities for Pharaoh. But the more they were oppressed, the more they multiplied and spread; so the Egyptians came to dread the Israelites and worked them ruthlessly. They made their lives bitter with hard labor in brick and mortar and with all kinds of work in the fields; in all their hard labor the Egyptians used them ruthlessly. (Exodus 1:6–13)

Joseph knew, even at the time of his own death, that his family would need eventually to return to their land. Here is the account:

Joseph stayed in Egypt, along with all his father's family. He lived a hundred and ten years and saw the third generation of Ephraim's children. Also the children of Makir son of Manasseh were placed at birth on Joseph's knees.

Then Joseph said to his brothers, "I am about to die. But God will surely come to your aid and take you up out of this land to the land he promised on oath to Abraham, Isaac and Jacob." And Joseph made the Israelites swear an oath and said, "God will surely come to your aid, and then you must carry my bones up from this place."

So Joseph died at the age of a hundred and ten. And after they embalmed him, he was placed in a coffin in Egypt. (Genesis 50:22–26)

Why did his brothers and their family stay in this land rather than return to the land God had promised to them? They moved to Egypt only temporarily during the famine, but apparently they got comfortable and stayed on. Sometimes we can also get trapped by our comfort. So we could say the negative result was due to the Israelites' own inaction. But I find that explanation a bit too easy, too much built on hindsight.

There is another way to see this result that offers a powerful reminder to each person in business, indeed each business today: even the best plans are only temporary. Winston Churchill said, "Success is not final, failure is not fatal: it is the courage to continue that counts." We should not be surprised when even a good plan does not continue to produce good value.

All that is needed to verify this point is to look at the top 500 companies in the United States in 1910, or even later. How many of these are among the top companies today? What has happened to International Harvester, Sunbeam, Merrill Lynch, McDonnell Douglas, Control Data Corporation, and a host of others? A&P was a grocery chain in the top five of companies in the 1950s and is completely gone today. Jagdish Sheth writes in *Self-Destructive Habits of Good Companies*, "Although it is commonly believed that institutions are (at least potentially) immortal and humans are mortal, I found that the average life span of corporations is declining, even as that of humans is rising."[1]

Ever since sin came into the world, we have seen deterioration. Whether we're looking at human lives or institutions or nations, the good times don't roll forever. In businesses, this deterioration sometimes comes from a management transition where a new plan is put in place. Sometimes it comes from external sources, when even a good plan cannot stand up to changes in the environment. Here are some illustrations of each of these situations.

We heard earlier from Wayne Alderson, the Pittron Steel Company vice president who demonstrated servant leadership in his approach to dealing with the labor unions. His leadership work resulted in his being named "Man of the Year" for labor in the state of Pennsylvania, the only person from the management side ever to receive this award. I asked Wayne what had happened to Pittron Steel:

> Pittron Steel had become so successful, it was sold, and with new management came new management ways. They liked the numbers but they didn't like our way of getting them. No more office for the union president. No more walking around on the

floor with the people. The new management said, "We don't want you doing this anymore."

I was called in to meet with the new owners. After much discussion I finally said, "Maybe your problem is that you need to make the rest of your company like Pittron instead of trying to make us like all of you." He reconfirmed his thinking, "We want the results, but you have to do it our way. If you don't, I will let you go." I was this close to saying yes, but I couldn't. I said, "No." He was asking me not just to compromise, but capitulate everything I stood for. I honestly believe he was sad.

It took seven years for Pittron to close, but indeed it closed forever. Thankfully, the Value of the Person [an organization rooted in the ideas we developed at Pittron] did not close with it. It lives on to this day.[2]

Wayne Alderson's work laid the groundwork for a profitable company. That it failed seven years after he left is not surprising. The world changed, a new plan was introduced, and the new plan failed. In this case, the ultimate failure of the company could be attributed to the new management's failure to understand the real reasons for its previous success. Success at one time, however, is no guarantee it will continue.

But sometimes a business's failure is not attributable to bad management. Consider the case of Perry Bigelow, who was named "Home Builder of the Year" in the U.S. in 2005 for his innovation in the design and construction of sustainable communities. When the economic crisis shut down home building in 2008, he had nowhere to go. Here is what he told me in an interview in March 2009:

> We never wanted to take on outside investors that might have made us focus on profit rather than the quality of life we were trying to create. In 2005, we had about 60 employees. We grew slowly because we wanted to create long-term stable jobs. We have very careful hiring practices. We believe it is important for people to make a commitment to a company that enables them to flourish. We try to make sure people have a clear vision

of the kind of company they are getting into. We walk them through the vision and mission statements to make sure they are a good fit for our culture.

In 2005, most of our people had been here for ten years or longer. We want to provide a stable working environment for people who want to have a balanced life. Our employees have three weeks of vacation after five years. If they maintain a B average, we pay the costs of their business-related education. One person working for us became a CPA. We offer health insurance, a 401k plan, and other benefits. We have always tried to advertise truthfully. When we advertise energy-efficient homes, they have to be energy efficient. When we market a community as child friendly, it has to be child friendly. Honesty in marketing drives you to excellence—no one wants to advertise they're average. Our largest community is HomeTown in Aurora, Illinois, with 1,288 homes; about 1,250 are completed. In 2005, we were building between 200 and 250 houses per year.

We are part of a benchmark group of private builders like ourselves, and we share data with each other three times per year. Through this information sharing, we began to prepare for the housing downturn in late 2005. We were handling it pretty well at first. In fact, we were profitable through 2007. Jamie, my son, has been doing the day-to-day leadership. I am more an idea person, and he is more the natural leader, and I admire his work greatly. But no one was prepared for what followed. What happened in October 2008 is what has really been destructive. With the sudden collapse of the financial market, all of our assets were devalued, which inhibited borrowing. But banks aren't lending to real estate regardless of your assets. So you are dependent on cash. In this business, you don't keep a lot of cash sitting around.

We are in the position now where we are chewing through what little cash we had. Sales basically stopped in the fourth quarter. We had had forty sales in the fourth quarter of 2005, and had two sales in the fourth quarter of 2008. It has been absolutely devastating. We are now down to about thirteen people. Until a year ago, most of the employee losses were due to attrition. But in the last year, we have had to do some layoffs. We simply had no choice.

About eighteen months ago, the first thing we did was to bring into our office the work we had been subbing out [hiring others to do]. This worked for about a year, but as the decline continued we had to take other steps. Every month Jamie discusses with our people what is going on. We have focused on preserving integrity while keeping the business going. We broke opportunities and problems down into teams, each working on a different part of the business. People became involved in finding ways to save money, looking for innovation. This has happened right up to the present time.[3]

And Bigelow Homes was not the only company feeling the brunt of the economic downturn. Flow Automotive, discussed in earlier chapters, is an exemplary auto company that was devastated by the downturn in the automobile business in late 2008. Here is what Don Flow said about how his business dealt with the economic downturn:

> We pulled people together into small groups and asked the question: What is it as a business that we are deeply committed to? What would we never go away from as a business? We concluded together that our service ethic, grounded in respect and truthfulness, was fundamental. If we lost that we would not have a reason to exist. Secondly, we concluded we must maintain an environment where we treat each other with respect. We have to have a fully participative environment where everyone is fully invested in what we are doing.
>
> From that foundation, we agreed to look at everything else and opened up the question of what we can change. A crisis truly galvanizes thinking and some great suggestions came forward. Perhaps these could have been implemented before, but they weren't. The crisis forced us to think differently and overcome inertia. We framed everything with three questions: Does it provide better service to customers? Does it enable our people to be more productive? Does it eliminate waste? Some great cost-saving suggestions came out, making us wonder how we made money before without dealing with these things! We tried things. We tested things. We made great progress. And we managed in doing this to avoid getting paralyzed, which can often happen in this kind of a situation.

> I realized I had to rethink my own job. I had the responsibility to bring hope and facts to the organization. If we were to move forward, we had to bring value to the customer and focus on our purpose.[4]

These external factors could have brought an end to Flow Automotive, as was the case with so many other businesses during the Great Recession of 2008. But even though they made it through and came out healthy on the other side, their business was in jeopardy because of external circumstances.

This same deterioration can happen on a much smaller scale. It does not necessarily impact only decisions made by the whole company. For example, I had decided, with my staff, that we did not need special executive parking privileges by our building at Boeing. Sometimes there is a case to be made for such privileges when executive management is constantly traveling to other locations and needs to efficiently get in and out of the building. But in our case, many of our researchers did the same, and we had adequate parking not too far away, so we decided we didn't need this perk.

That decision, however, was not enough. We needed to convince both my management and the facilities department, who had standards for such things. The process took six months and we celebrated, along with research staff, the painting out of the "red squares" that indicated executive-only parking. A few years later, after I had left the company, I was invited back to give a talk in the building. All of the red squares had returned. As with Pittron Steel and so many other good companies, good ideas don't endure without careful tending.

In light of all of this modern experience, we should not be surprised at the deterioration of Joseph's plan that, at the time, saved the world from starvation. I find this explanation for the breakdown at the end of the story the most compelling of the alternatives.

That Joseph's plan did not last does not mean he failed in his work, and it provides insight for our own work. We could take the direction that so many Christians do and assume that nothing we do here on this earth will last. All of it will be swept away in the final judgment, so that is just the way it is.

But there is another way of viewing our struggle against deterioration in our work. Darrel Cosden in *The Heavenly Good of Earthly Work*, N. T. Wright in *Surprised by Hope: Rethinking Heaven, the Resurrection, and the Mission of the Church*, and Eugene Peterson in *Practice Resurrection: A Conversation on Growing Up in Christ* all argue persuasively that looking to the end times as a time when everything here will be taken away is not the only way to read Scripture.[5] Rather, they suggest, we should be working under God's authority now for the ushering in of the new kingdom here on earth. They do not suggest that things will endure without a struggle until the new kingdom comes. The deterioration we all face in our work will still be present. But their insight can add purpose and hope to our work.

Regardless of our own views, there is no room for being pessimistic or giving up, in spite of the reality of deterioration. We are called by God, as we will see in the next chapter, to carry on this work, including our work in business. We must do it well and with purpose because God calls us to do so. Obedience to him should be all the motivation we need. In this sense, Joseph, Don Flow, Perry Bigelow, and Wayne Alderson should inspire us to do our own work in this way.

Though Joseph's work saved the world from starvation at the time, we should not be surprised at the deterioration of what Joseph set out to do, or even of what we do. This is what sin has done to the world. Good ideas need to be tended. Sometimes, as circumstances change, what was a good idea in the past no longer is effective. In order for a leader to continue to bring hope, a good purpose requires attention to ward off deterioration, and looking out to see what needs to be changed.

26

THE CORPORATE STORY

In Exodus 1:8 we read, "And there arose a Pharaoh who did not know about Joseph." Through his connection to God and his great insight, Joseph had saved both the people of Egypt and the empire for Pharaoh. But he had been forgotten. The people of Israel were now a threat to the nation of Egypt and no one seemed to remember why they were there. Their enslavement and forced hard labor threatened their very existence, but it led to the great exodus from that land with long-term consequences for Egypt as well. The lack of a story caused considerable difficulty for Joseph's descendants.

Philosopher George Santayana warned that "those who cannot remember the past are condemned to repeat it." An important solution to this problem is a company record and a commitment to telling stories to keep those difficult times in mind. In her book *Around the Corporate Campfire: How Great Leaders Use Stories to Inspire Success*, Evelyn Clark makes the case in her introduction:

> Great leaders know that workers need more than lofty mission statements and industry buzzwords. To understand and appreciate what their organization stands for, workers need to hear about its people, its values, and its history. So smart leaders tell stories. . . . By touching the hearts as well as the minds of their employees, customers, and stakeholders, they leave a legacy of experiences that inspire generations.[1]

Stories represent an important dimension of business communications. We will consider several types of examples here.

David J. McIntyre Jr. is president and CEO of TriWest Healthcare Alliance, a collection of nonprofit health insurance plans and university hospital systems that initially focused on military personnel. He told me that his business had committed to act with integrity even if it cost them something. To illustrate what this meant for their company, he told the story of a time when they were in the middle of negotiations for a major contract extension and needed to make a decision about a loss of customer data.

> On December 14, 2002, thieves broke into one of our offices and stole hard drives containing the personal data on over 500,000 customers—members of the military, retired military, and their family members. Everyone from privates to four-star generals and admirals, including the chairman of the Joint Chiefs of Staff—that's a pretty daunting list. We obviously were concerned about protecting our customers from the criminals using that information for identity theft. There were also people who were concerned about whether the information was stolen for potential blackmail material against the government.
>
> We asked ourselves, "If our name was in that database, what would we want to have done?" The experts said that the only thing you could do is to contact your customers within seven to ten days so they can take steps to protect themselves. So that's what we did. It took a couple of days to build a communications campaign, and then we went fully public. Although we didn't exactly want the notoriety, we went to the news media to ask their help in getting the message out across the country. All the networks, the *New York Times*, the *Wall Street Journal*, and others carried it as a lead story. Our goal was to try and reach people, regardless of where they were located in preparation for the holidays.[2]

Would their opponent use this against them in the negotiation? They did. Would the government question their competence for the new contract? Perhaps. But the government customer also saw the integrity with which they addressed this important issue, and in the end TriWest won the contract they were pursuing. They continue to use this story internally to help newer employees understand what integrity means in their company.

Wayne Alderson, whom I have mentioned extensively in earlier chapters, had an ordinary career as a financial officer for ten years at Pittron Steel near Pittsburgh, until the plant was faced with a violent strike. It was then that he received the call to become vice president of operations.

> There were a lot of good things about Pittron, but even with those, it was still a hellhole because of the hatred that union and management had for each other. And then there was the union president, Sam Piccolo, a man who truly hated management as well. The strike he led was ugly, long, and threatened to take the company under. Even then, however, I was drawn to the plight of the workers, thinking about the men without paychecks and a Christmas without presents for the kids.[3]

Wayne's response to this crisis became the foundation for his "Value of the Person" philosophy that we discussed in chapter 3. He created a cleaner, lighter workplace. He built a positive relationship with the union president, seeking to demonstrate his value as an individual and the value of his position. He learned the names of his employees, even thanking them at the end of the day for a good day's work. This became a life story for Wayne, who worked on labor management relationships for the rest of his life. Wherever he went, he told the story of the miracle at Pittron and how it changed the lives of the workers and created success for the company.

One of the most widely known corporate stories involves Johnson & Johnson. On September 29, 1982, a twelve-year-old girl from the Chicago area died after taking an Extra Strength Tylenol capsule. By October 1, six more people from the Chicago area had died after taking Tylenol. After discovering the link to Tylenol in all cases, the Chicago area police broadcast warnings about taking the product. Johnson & Johnson responded to the news by distributing warnings to hospitals and distributors, while halting production and advertising. On October 5, Johnson & Johnson issued a nationwide recall of Tylenol products, pulling thirty-one million bottles of Tylenol with a retail value of over $100 million from the shelves.

I had known about this incident for years, but when I had the opportunity to meet with Ralph Larsen, a retired CEO from Johnson & Johnson, I wanted a bit more of the story (Jim Burke was the CEO at the time of the incident). I asked Ralph whether there was ever a discussion about simply pulling Tylenol from the shelves in only certain locations, or if this was a strategy to gain the confidence of the nationwide public and preserve the Tylenol brand. He said:

> No one ever asked what the cost would be. It was not in the decision-making process. Whatever the cost would be, that's what it would be. No one sat down and said, if we recall it from six states it will be this much, eight states it will cost this much, etc. People's lives were at stake. And at the end of the discussion, Jim Burke simply said, "I want every bottle off the shelf."
>
> The common wisdom in the room was that this was the end of the product. No one strategized whether this would be the best for the brand. If Jim were here, he would say, "At every point in the decision-making process, the only question we asked ourselves was what is in the public interest? And if the public interest was to recall everything, that would be the decision."[4]

Johnson & Johnson has a company credo that supports these decision processes. In summary, it states: Our first responsibility is to our customers, including doctors and nurses, and all the people who use our products. Our second responsibility is to our employees, including paying fair wages and doing what is right by them. Our third responsibility is to be good corporate citizens. Our last responsibility is to the shareholder. But if you do well by the first three, the shareholders do very well. The story illustrated the credo at a time when the financial impact was high. "We extracted lessons from the case," said Ralph, "and they have become part of the training of the whole company." So much so, in fact, that Ralph could tell the story of the previous CEO's decision as if it were his own. More than thirty years later, the story lives on.

So one way a business can use a story is to record key events that tell how the company confronted a crisis in the past. It seems that the Egyptian royal line could have used a corporate storyteller.

But sometimes a story is best left untold. In Genesis 45, Joseph revealed himself to his brothers when they bowed down to him. The brothers bowed down to him again after their father died, when again they feared retribution would finally come. Again he offered forgiveness (Genesis 50). I wonder if he thought about reminding them of his dreams, and how they were now fulfilled. He could have used that time to gloat. We have all seen poor winners, who use the time of a victory to "rub it in." But we don't see that from Joseph. It may have been the hard times in slavery and in prison that created a level of humility in him, but this is a good thing. Similarly, we may have stories of triumph that sound good, but wouldn't bring value.

Another way to use a story is to get past the defenses of the mind and communicate a message in a more subtle way. I was trained as a mathematician and remember saying to someone when I was in graduate school, "I wonder why there are all of those stories in the Bible? If a few principles were laid out, then we could figure out everything we need to know through a logical, rational argument." How foolish! It is clear that stories help us understand something in a way that is often less threatening and more nuanced than any logical argument.

In 2 Samuel 12, Nathan the prophet needed to confront King David about his moral failure. He could have confronted David directly, telling him of the wrong he had done. But David was a powerful ruler, and he had just used this power to have an affair with Bathsheba, the wife of his general Uriah. To add to his problem, when he found she was pregnant with his child he tried to cover it up by sending Uriah home to sleep with her. This way, everyone (including Uriah) would think the baby was his. When that didn't work, David sent him into the frontlines of battle and had the men fall back so that Uriah would be killed. Essentially he committed adultery and covered it up with murder. He was not about to listen to anything from a prophet.

Rather than directly confronting David, Nathan told him a story about a rich man with many sheep and a neighboring poor man with one pet lamb. When the rich man had dinner guests, rather than take one of his own sheep for the main course, he took and killed the poor man's pet lamb. When he asked David what should be done with that rich man, David responded, "Any man who would do such a thing deserves to die!" Nathan then said to him, "You are that man!"

We can therefore add storytelling to the toolbox of communicating with people in authority, a subject we considered in chapter 12. As a slight variation on this theme, we often tell stories to explain complex ideas. I frequently found myself explaining new technology to executives at Boeing through stories or analogies. Thomas Kuhn, in his book *The Structures of Scientific Revolutions*, describes science in this way: A theory is developed to explain the world as it is, and then discoveries are made that no longer fit the theory or the story. This causes the scientists to either explain the data or create a new theory.[5] Interestingly, C. S. Lewis follows the same path, without scientific or mathematical language, in his remarkable book *The Discarded Image: An Introduction to Medieval and Renaissance Literature*. He traces the way people through the ages have captured their understanding of the world through stories, and when the story no longer fits the world, it is modified.[6]

A touch of humor added to the story can also help cement an idea. Gloria Nelund uses a story in this way to explain how she dealt with being the only woman in a two-hundred-person executive team when she was the president of the Deutsche Bank Capital Assets Management of America division:

> There was one time earlier in my career when I was a part of a larger staff of all men. When the conversation got heated, they would sometimes leave the room and go to the bathroom. When they returned they would have a solution to the issue we were dealing with. But they did this once too often. On the next occasion, I followed them into the men's bathroom. They never did that again.[7]

Dallas Willard, in his book *Hearing God*, encourages us to look at the stories of the Bible in this way:

> If we are really to understand the Bible record, we must enter into our study of it on the assumption that the experiences recorded there are basically of the same type as ours would have been if we had been there. Those who lived through those experiences felt very much as we would have if we had been in their place.[8]

By looking carefully at the story of Joseph, we gain insight into our own careers. We can enter his life and see how he handled important issues in order to learn about ourselves. It is in this way that we have been using the story of Joseph. Though he lived in a different time and place, we can learn basic lessons on business, faith, and calling through reliving his story.

Thus stories can help us remember key times in our history, cut though our defenses to gain new insight, and create a picture that helps us understand a complex topic. We have tried to use the story of Joseph in all these ways.

27

CALLING

We have considered many individual moments in the life of Joseph, so let's look at the totality of his life. Working people frequently ask, "Is my work meaningful?" Joseph might have asked the same question as he reflected back on all that had happened to him. At the end of the food project in Egypt, in conversation with his brothers, who were afraid of his retribution after their father had died, Joseph said, "You intended to harm me, but God intended it for good to accomplish what is now being done, the saving of many lives" (Genesis 50:20). Not only did he see that his work was meaningful ("the saving of many lives"), but it was also in response to the call of God ("God intended it for good"). Can we say this about our own work?

In a larger sense, calling is about our whole lives, not just our work, though it certainly includes our work. In his book *The Call: Finding and Fulfilling the Central Purpose of Your Life*, Os Guinness asserts that our "primary calling is by [God], to him, and for him." Our secondary calling is that "everyone, everywhere, and in everything should think, speak, live, and act entirely for him. . . . If all that a believer does grows out of faith and is done for the glory of God, then all dualistic distinctions are demolished. There is no higher/lower, sacred/secular . . . or first class/second class. . . . The business person, the teacher, the factory worker, and the television anchor—can do God's work (or fail to do it) just as much as the minister or missionary."[1]

Readers wanting to pursue this bigger topic would do well to consider some of the excellent resources on this subject.[2] For this chapter we will focus on that aspect of calling in our daily work, learning from Joseph and others how they saw their work under God. It is in this part of the discussion that we are often confused about what kind of work God might call us to do.

Many young people today look for a career choice that offers the right combination of meaningful work and a good compensation package to go with it. But even with these criteria, the outcome of such decisions is not always favorable. In *Saving the Corporate Soul & (Who Knows) Maybe Your Own*, David Batstone writes, "Corporate workers from the mail room to the highest executive offices express dissatisfaction with their work. They feel crushed by the widespread greed, selfishness, and quest for profit at any cost."[3]

How did Joseph achieve career satisfaction and a true sense of calling? In reality, he was close to the position of the many people in the world who have no career choice. For them it is not a question of meaningful work, but a question of work at all. He didn't get to do a skills inventory, choose his university, and then interview for a variety of positions that would provide the best outcome. He worked for his father, worked as a slave, worked in prison, and finally was appointed to his position as CEO of the Egyptian International Food Company by Pharaoh, without any real opportunity to make a decision. He could never have said, "I decline the position because I like my other options better."

But he did indeed make important decisions along the way. He chose to remain connected to his God. He chose to have a good attitude about his work, even work that most would regard as undesirable. In all of his positions, though he had little choice about *what* he did, he did choose *how* he would do it. I believe these are the keys to his ability to bring meaning to his work. A likely apocryphal story from the Middle Ages illustrates this point. Two men were doing the same job, hauling rocks at a construction site. The first one said, "I hate my job. All I do is move rocks all day and it is difficult, hot, and dirty work." The second one said, "I love my job. I am building a cathedral." Perspective makes a huge difference in our work.

Barry Rowan, the chief financial officer of Cool Planet Energy Systems, went through a process of understanding meaning and purpose for his own career.

> I came to see that I had been thinking about work all wrong and mostly backward. I had to be taken through a succession of paradigm shifts. For example, I was looking at work from the outside in rather than from the inside out. I thought if I just got the right job I would be happy. I spent the first ten years of my career wondering what I should do for my career.
>
> It was through that process that I concluded that we don't derive meaning from our work; rather, we bring meaning to our work. It is the perspective of our work that brings meaning to it. For any job, we can bring either a life-draining or a life-giving perspective to that work. Take a hospice worker, for example, like the one who took care of my mother-in-law. I could describe that job as changing bedpans for a living for people who are going to die anyway. Or I could view the work as creating an environment of unconditional love for God's people in the last few precious months of their lives. Even with the life-giving perspective, you still have to change the bedpans, but it is with a radically different way of understanding what you are doing.
>
> As I came to see this distinction, it became incumbent on me to articulate a life-giving perspective of my job as a CFO, as a business leader. For years I couldn't do it. Not honestly and in a way that inspired me anyway. But as I wrestled through the question, my understanding grew and my perspective shifted. I realized that I had also listened to the clamor of the culture that says, "We are what we do," instead of seeing the deeper truth that says, "What we do is an expression of who we are." Through this struggle, I stumbled on a working job definition for myself, which is "to contribute to a better society as seen through the eyes of God." That in turn led to the understanding that the fundamental purpose of business is to serve.[4]

Even though he had a successful career by outward standards, Barry had to do some soul-searching to discover the meaning in his work.

Sometimes a good boss can also help workers see the meaning and purpose in their work. Bill Pollard, CEO of ServiceMaster, had workers in his employ who did dirty jobs. Among other things, they cleaned the floors, bathrooms, and toilets in the hospitals where ServiceMaster worked. So Pollard found ways to help them connect their work with purpose.

> Their job is not just to clean the floor, their job is to help that patient become well. So the purpose of their work extends beyond the task. In our hospital services, we would often ask nurses or doctors to meet with our people and talk with them about how important their work was to the health of the patient.[5]

In this way they were able to bring meaning to their work.

At Boeing, we used to try to help our people see their work from a bigger perspective. In 1986 when the 767 airplane first rolled out, we put up a large poster of the airplane on the bulletin board in the coffee room and attached names and projects to the various parts of the airplane our employees had created. People could see that they contributed to the end product, whether by designing a new surface-fitting method to create a smooth join between the wing and the body, a flight-planning algorithm for the cockpit, or the electronic system onboard the airplane. In a similar way, we took our employees to the factory to see the airplanes being built, providing a picture of how everyone was contributing through their work, from advanced algorithms to administrative support.

By contrast, in a recent conversation with a nephew in the Navy, he described a naval exercise he was on for five months. He had no idea why they were going to certain locations or what they accomplished by being there. All he had were the day-to-day tasks associated with the voyage and nothing to provide motivation for why they did what they did. He said it led to a certain resignation that was not supportive of people putting their whole hearts into their work or seeing any meaning in it. I am certain many jobs are like this, and it can indeed be frustrating.

Another problem in considering career and vocation is to give too much credence to public perception. In 2006, *Forbes* produced a report with the public's ranking of "most admired professions." Here is the list in order of the report's findings:

1. Firefighter	13. Athlete
2. Doctor	14. Lawyer
3. Nurse	15. Entertainer
4. Scientist	16. Accountant
5. Teacher	17. Banker
6. Military officer	18. Journalist
7. Police officer	19. Union leader
8. Clergy	20. Actor
9. Farmer	21. Business executive
10. Engineer	22. Stockbroker
11. Member of Congress	23. Real estate agent
12. Architect	

Of the business executive, the *Forbes* study commented, "No profession is demonized more in the entertainment world: It's tough to earn respect when movies and network shows incessantly portray 'greedy businessmen' as villains of the plot."[6]

Yet Joseph's career in business was not only meaningful for him but also meaningful for the world. Part of the difficulty in bringing meaning and purpose to business comes when business leaders lose sight of the important role that business plays in the community and focus instead only on how much money they can make. This is compounded by how leaders view profit, focusing on weekly or quarterly gains and not on the longer term. With no greater purpose, workers at the executive level focus on anything that will improve the bottom line, which can create instability and meaninglessness for those in the lower ranks.

Obviously, profit is critical for any business. Without it, the business would not be sustainable and would not contribute to the flourishing of the community. But when this becomes the sole goal, it fails. Don Flow put it this way:

> We have to have a profit to do the things a business needs to do. If you do not create value for capital you are actually destroying wealth. An organization shouldn't exist if it is destroying society's wealth. I don't know a healthy person who gets up in the morning and looks in the mirror and says, "I live for my blood." But I don't know a person alive who does not have blood. Blood is like profit—necessary to live but not the reason for living.[7]

When we lose sight of the big things we are doing and replace those things only with money, we distort our purpose. Ironically, when we do this and it is felt throughout the organization, people are less productive and the company may undermine its ability to make money!

Many Christians believe that in order to be in "full-time Christian service," they must work as a pastor or a missionary or at least in a faith-based organization. Some extend this to an imagined hierarchy of jobs for Christians that might look like this:

1. Missionary	6. Doctor
2. Pastor	7. Scientist
3. Parachurch worker	8. Engineer
4. Nurse/teacher	9. Lawyer
5. Nonprofit worker	10. Business executive

The work in "full-time Christian service" comes first. The professions of nursing and teaching are near the top of the list because, although they are not "full-time Christian," they are relatively low paid and help people. Higher-paid professions are jobs but certainly not callings. Higher-paid professions are seen as important only because they enable a person to have money to support Christian ministries, or perhaps to witness to non-Christians in their work settings. Lawyers and businesspeople are low on the list because of all of the scandals common in these professions.

Being a missionary is a wonderful profession, and God calls some to do that work. The same can be said for pastors, nurses, and teachers. But what about a career in business for a Christian? Bonnie Wurzbacher, senior vice president of Coca-Cola, had a career journey with some similarities to Joseph's story. She didn't have to endure the hardships of jail and slavery, but she did have to face up to the stereotype of a career in business. Here is her story:

> I was raised in a Christian community. My father was a minister, my grandparents were missionaries, my great-grandfather was a minister, my uncle was a minister, and I went to a Christian school. I grew up spending more time in our church than I did in my high school. I became a victim of thinking that you have to find meaningful work: If there is meaningful work then there is non-meaningful work. And if there is meaningful work it's full-time Christian work or maybe not-for-profit work (as if just being in a particular job means you are honoring God). Not-for-profit work is meaningful and socially responsible.

> Well, I have learned and now would argue that for-profit work is equally meaningful because all that other work can't happen without it and because the actual work itself glorifies God. Many people want to do good in the world but they have the perception that only not-for-profit work or certain "full-time Christian work" is meaningful work. According to this view if you are in business, that's not meaningful work; work in business is about getting a paycheck and doing the job ethically.

> So, that's the first notion you have to get out of your head and realize that it's God who commands us to honor him with our heart, mind, soul, and strength, and that pretty much covers it

all in all work. So I think, the way we come to work needs to and already does fulfill the Great Commandment.

Work is an opportunity to fulfill the Creation Mandate. When the world was created, the Creation Mandate was laid out in Genesis 1:27–28. Being fruitful and multiplying and subduing the earth is about building the social world, not just families. It includes cities, schools, and countries. It includes harnessing the creativity and the power that God created into this earth through every single thing that we do. I think that was a call to honor God in every aspect of our lives including our work.

Work gives us a way to fulfill the Great Commission because it brings us straight out into the world every day with people from all walks of life, in a way that wouldn't happen if you worked in your own home in an agrarian culture. It forces us to engage with the world at large and to be God's salt and light and love in the world.

I think that once I came to realize I could serve God in business, I still thought it was mostly about ethics and evangelism. I do think it's about ethics, and I think that there are some very big ethical challenges for senior executives and for the everyday worker. My experience related to evangelism is that the times when I was able to share my faith in meaningful ways was through relationships with people, whether at home or work and often when they are going through crisis. Well, that's a minute amount of my time compared with how much time I spend at work. So, it has to be more than that.

What I've learned is that it is also through the product and the process of our work that we honor God. It's doing what we do with excellence—being an excellent marketer, an excellent salesperson, or an excellent teacher—and working at that as if God was your boss. You would do it in a way that is ethical and sustainable and high quality because you are doing this as unto him.[8]

More than a job. More than an opportunity to witness. More than ethics. All of these are important, but they are not the call to business. For Joseph, this call also included the product of his work. Bonnie said this as well. Perhaps it is easy to see how storing and saving grain is important for our world, but making Coca-Cola products? I asked her about that, and here is her response:

> I say the purpose of business is first to advance the economic well-being of communities around the world and secondly to enable every other institution to exist. Without sustainable ethical wealth creation, the world doesn't work. One of the things we are seeing in this economy is how interrelated it all is. As jobs go away, the tax base goes away and the government budget deficit rises. Now, we are seeing not-for-profits and churches hugely impacted because the sustainable wealth creation stream is at least temporarily broken in some areas.
>
> Now, you asked about the product. The first thing is that no company survives without products and services that people need and want. If you don't have that, you have nothing. So, nothing works long term without a basic value proposition that is needed or wanted in the world and I think that's where we have seen some of the major problems: One is when there is an ethical problem; two is when the basic fundamental need or desire for that product or service goes away (or was smoke and mirrors in the case of some businesses).
>
> So, yes, products and services are really important, because if they are not needed and wanted business is not sustainable. As it relates to Coca-Cola, you can think: If you look at the alternatives to that around the world, the alternatives in many places are unclean water. One of the first things you see when people begin to move out of poverty into the middle class is a desire for more convenient products. They have enough wealth to be able to change their life from being focused just on their own sustainability—for example, spending their whole time going to collect water—to actually being able to do something else with their life and to generate businesses.[9]

She sees a value in the product (both convenience and safe refreshment) and a value in the economic opportunity the product creates for individuals and communities. Her commitment to delivering this value gets her going each morning. Like Joseph, she sees a big purpose in what she is doing, tied directly to the call of God on her life.

Somehow, many Christians have lost sight of the Creation Mandate (described in Genesis 1–2 as one of our purposes as humans) to develop, explore, and continue the work God has commissioned them to do. Some have replaced this by making everything physical in this world secondary to otherworldly, spiritual things. When I was teaching on this in Africa, a pastor asked me, "Which is more important: to teach people to believe in Jesus, or to develop disciples to carry out his work here in this world?" I told him that I used to work for an airplane company and that his question was like asking my designers, "Which wing is more important for flight, the left wing or the right wing?" Like an airplane that requires both wings, in our lives as believers we are called both to accept Christ and to follow him in the world.

God has many things for us to do and has gifted each of us differently for different kinds of work. There are those called to be pastors and missionaries, scientists and engineers, teachers and medical professionals, and businesspeople and lawyers. Whatever our vocation, we need to respond to God with the talents and abilities he has given us, working together to act as his hands and feet in the world.

Sometimes it is simply a matter of opportunity. Then, like Joseph, we get to work as well as we can in whatever it is we do. This is what Paul told the Colossians when he wrote, "Whatever you do, work at it with all your heart, as working for the Lord and not for men. . . . It is the Lord Christ you are serving" (Colossians 3:23–24).

Joseph was raised in a family that—going back to his great-grandfather Abraham, his grandfather Isaac, and his father Jacob—was called to be a light for God in the world. But when it came to his daily work, we see the wealth this work produced for Jacob. He did it cleverly. Yes, he gave 10 percent back to God. But we do not see anything to indicate he saw this work having intrinsic value. It appeared to be primarily a means to another end. By contrast, Joseph knew that his work saved lives.

It is clear, however, that Joseph was called by God to do his daily work—and that work is most closely interpreted in a modern setting as the role of a business executive. Not a business executive in a "religious company," but rather a business leader in a difficult environment. Yet before God elevated him to right-hand man to Pharaoh, Joseph had to endure slavery and prison—both of which were a part of his career path, which also served to take off the edge of his arrogance and prepare him for his leadership work in the food industry.

While he didn't have many choices, he didn't just take everything passively. He had a dream. He had motivation. He sent a message to Pharaoh when he was wrongly accused. And he applied himself in whatever opportunity he had, keeping his connection with God. But it is fair to say that his work for his father, his work in Potiphar's house, and his work in the prison were all also work that he did well before God. No matter where we are, each of us can find a part of Joseph's career to which we can relate.

Whatever our own circumstances, at the top of an organization or at the bottom, the career of Joseph provides a helpful perspective for responding to our own vocational call. While he wasn't perfect, he kept his connection with God, worked hard and honorably regardless of his position, and brought a sense of meaning and purpose to his work.

28

FINAL REFLECTIONS

Over the past fifteen years I have had the opportunity to interview over one hundred leaders, primarily from business. I have quoted from many of them in this book. Although they come from both public and private companies, all have attributes critical to shaping what I think good business should look like in the twenty-first century. These conversations in their entirety are available at www.ethix.org.

To prepare for each of these interviews, I researched the company and the individual, looking at their recorded stories. I looked for places where the public accounts don't address the issues I was curious about, and I created a set of questions to discuss with the business leader.

For example, there is the well-known story of Johnson & Johnson, the company that pulled Tylenol from the shelves across the country after six people died in the early 1980s (see chapter 26). After reading many accounts, I wondered whether this was a strategy to gain market confidence, or whether it was done out of concern for the public. Since I couldn't find any record of this, I met with former CEO Ralph Larsen and asked him about it.

Generally, I discussed these questions with a colleague to gain another perspective, and when possible I took a colleague along with me on the interview. For the first five years of publishing *Ethix*, David Gill and I conducted these interviews together. Many others have participated in them since.

But I wish I could have an interview with Joseph! Even after researching the story carefully, there are so many places where I would like to know more. Here are some of the questions I would ask him:

- Looking back, do you think your attitude contributed to your conflict with your brothers in the early days? Why did you wear that multicolored coat when you went looking for your brothers at your father's direction?

- Did you have any second thoughts about the encounter with Potiphar's wife? Was there any other approach you might have taken?

- When you were in prison for that long period of time, it is evident you were able to maintain your relationship with God. But were there any people who encouraged you as the years passed? Did you ever get depressed or discouraged?

- When you told Pharaoh the meaning of his dream, how were you thinking about your own future? Were you worried that your ideas would be taken by others and that you would go back to prison?

- In setting up the business to collect and distribute grain, how did you do your hiring? What training did you provide for your employees? What was your management style? Did you pay people well?

- During the fourteen years of the business, did you ever wonder if your understanding of the interpretation of the dream might be incorrect? What if the famine had not started after seven years?

- Why do you think, during those seven plentiful years while you were collecting grain, that others around you didn't also save for the future? Were there any warning signs that they might also run out of money and become wards of the state?

- Did you consider an alternative to forcing those who couldn't pay for food into slavery? What thinking went into this decision?

- Your brothers had treated you horribly, and in the end you were gracious about it. But what was your motivation for the deceptive tests? When I suggested that it was to test their trustworthiness, did I understand you correctly?

- With all of the money, power, and authority you had, did you ever abuse your position? Did you get used to the surroundings and forget what the average person's life was like? On reflection, is there anything you would do differently now?

- Did you ever remind your brothers about the dreams you told them about when you were seventeen years old?

- When the world was saved from starvation and the famine ended, what was your role?

- Why did you and your family stay in Egypt after the famine ended? Did you consider returning home with your family at this point? After seeing the long-term result, would you do it differently?

- Amid a foreign culture a long way from home, surrounded by power and prestige, how did you remain connected with God? It doesn't seem that you had a group of people around you to hold you accountable.

I'm sure you must have your own questions and that you would appreciate joining in on the interview! Unfortunately, however, we don't have the opportunity—at least in this life—to have this discussion with Joseph. We have access only to the text in Genesis 37–50, and numerous commentaries on it. Because I don't know the answers to many of these questions, I have tried in most cases to stop short of speculation and only comment on what I know of the story.

David Brooks writes in *The Social Animal*,

> [As Harold reread a book,] he noticed entirely different points and arguments. . . . Either he or the book had changed. What had happened, of course, is that as he had done more reading he had unconsciously reorganized the information in his brain.[1]

This statement captures my thoughts about the story of Joseph. From the time I was a child I have read and reread this story. But after a career in business, and a post-career in the academy looking at issues at the intersection of business and faith, I now see the account differently than I did as a child. It is these new impressions of the story of Joseph that I have laid out in this book.

I wrote the second complete draft of this book from a rental house in the Los Angeles area in March 2012. During breaks from writing—in addition to visiting with my wife, our daughter, and her family there—I was reading the biography *Steve Jobs* by Walter Isaacson. Jobs was a brilliant, insightful, and deeply flawed leader.[2] This powerful story challenged me to see that no human, other than Jesus, was a pure hero. But we can learn from many in spite of their weaknesses. This conclusion has helped me in the business interviews I have done over the years. People have asked me, "What if this person you interviewed fails?" And some have. The answer is that you can learn from a good practice whether the person continues in such practices or not.

This observation also caused me to look at the Joseph story a bit differently. He was human and he likely did stumble from time to time. This was quite clear in the arrogance he seemed to show early in his life, although it was less clear from the text in his later work. There are, of course, plenty of places to raise questions, and some of these I have raised above. But when we don't know the other side, we should be careful about rushing to judgment.

My British friend Paul Graves is a business and brand strategy consulting expert with a background in advertising. He used to work in the London agency scene, and he once described to me a TV commercial that was developed for *The Guardian*, a newspaper in the United Kingdom. The video opened with a picture of a "skinhead" running down the street and grabbing a business man with a briefcase in a threatening manner. But then the video took another angle on the scene. From the front, with a view that extended higher, it showed the same scene—except this time you could see a huge piece of construction scaffolding falling from the top of the building right where the man would have been. The tagline was, "*The Guardian*, a different point of view." Indeed, don't rush to judgment!

That said, I don't think Joseph was perfect, but I do believe there is much we can learn from what we know about his story— and much we would still like to know!

ACKNOWLEDGMENTS

Many people provided helpful counsel to me as I wrote this book. My son Michael read and commented on an earlier draft and offered good insight. Phillip Jap sat through a class I taught on an early draft, and then marked it up and discussed his insights with me. Miles Wray, a recent graduate from Seattle Pacific University, came looking for an internship while still a senior. He read the book, offering detailed comments and suggestions. My thanks also to Miles for preparing the index for this book. Ted Terry is a friend who works with publishers, and he provided encouragement and insight on the publishing process. I am also grateful to Hannah Brown and Patricia Anders from Hendrickson Publishers. They offered the ultimate balance of fine detailed comments on wording and the suggestions for reorganizing parts of the text. The book has greatly benefitted from their insights.

I am also grateful to each person who was willing to allow me to interview them over the past fifteen years. They have created the backstory for this book. Not all of them have been quoted, but all of them have had an influence. Many not only agreed to do the interview but then provided introductions for others, opening the door to yet another interview. Bill Pollard, Prabhu Guptara, and Roger Eigsti made several introductions. And there are many people who provided introductions to key people in their networks whom I would likely not have met on my own. David Gautschi, dean at the Graduate School of Business at Fordham University, opened many doors. So did Earl Palmer, pastor emeritus at University Presbyterian Church, who invited me to some CEO events at Laity Lodge in Texas, where I met a number of leaders. Howard Butt, who chaired these events, was an encourager and a friend.

Finally, I should mention just a few of the many key mentors in my life. Author Francis Schaeffer changed the way I thought about my faith by opening up a much bigger world to consider. Al Greene became a special mentor for many years. A founder of the Christian school my children attended, and a friend for many years later, he reshaped my way of thinking about the world, for which I am grateful. Wayne Alderson first modeled what it is to be a Christian in a business, and our friendship started soon after I heard him interviewed on the radio. I had met many Christians in business, in particular my father, who set great examples. But Wayne Alderson took this integration of his faith and his business deeper than I had encountered before. David Gill has been a thought-provoking friend and fellow teacher in many settings for many years and has pushed me as well.

My wife of over fifty years, Nancy, has been the true partner in this endeavor. Not only has she put up with the distractions of my time in writing this book, she has read the material, commented significantly, and then used it with a small group of working women she leads in a Bible study on connecting work and faith. Her red-penciled comments have not always been immediately received with joy, but they have made this book better.

My three children—Michael, Andrew, and Amy, and their spouses and children—are a vital part of my life and a deep part of this book.

Thanks to all.

LIST OF *ETHIX* INTERVIEWS

Over the past fifteen years I have been conducting extensive interviews with business and thought leaders, seeking to explore good business practices. I have drawn from a number of these interviews in this book, including the following. The complete text of these interviews and many others is available online at www.ethix.org.

Wayne Alderson, former vice president, Pittron Steel; founder, Value of the Person (July 2009)

Dennis Bakke, cofounder, former president, and CEO, AES; CEO, Imagine Schools (May 2004)

Steven J. Bell, owner and CEO, Pacific Crest Industries (July 2008)

Beverly Bothel, managing broker, Windermere Real Estate East, Bellevue, Washington (March 2009)

Perry Bigelow, owner and CEO, Bigelow Homes (March 2009)

Marshall N. Carter, deputy chair/director, NYSE Euronext Inc. (August 2010)

Don Flow, owner and CEO, Flow Automotive Companies (March 2004)

Prabhu Guptara, director, Organizational Development, UBS Wolfsberg (January 2004)

Tami Heim, partner, The A Group Brand Development; former president, Borders Books; former chief publishing officer, Thomas Nelson (January 2012)

Hsieh Fu Hua, CEO, Singapore Exchange Limited (December 2003)

Guy Kawasaki, cofounder, Alltop.com; managing director, Garage Technology Ventures; former Apple evangelist (October 2010)

Ralph Larsen, former CEO, Johnson & Johnson (June 2007)

Clive Mather, president and CEO, Shell of Canada Limited (December 2008)

Alan Mulally, president and CEO, Ford Motor Company (July 2010)

Gloria Nelund, CEO and cofounder, TriLink Global; former president, Deutsche Bank North America Private Wealth Management (March 2012)

Peter Pace, 16th chair, Joint Chiefs of Staff (September 2008)

Gregory R. Page, executive chairman of the board, Cargill (April 2010)

C. William Pollard, chairman emeritus, The ServiceMaster Company (September 2006)

John S. Reed, co-CEO (retired), Citigroup (March 2002)

Barry Rowan, CFO, Vonage (July 2011)

James P. Sinegal, CEO, Costco (March 2003)

Brad Tilden, chair and CEO, Alaska Air Group (May 2013)

Jack vanHartesvelt, executive vice president, Kennedy Associates, Westin Hotels (November 2012)

Sherron Watkins, former vice president of corporate development and whistleblower, Enron (May 2007)

Bonnie Wurzbacher, executive vice president, The Coca-Cola Company (December 2009)

Bibliography

Batstone, David. *Saving the Corporate Soul & (Who Knows) Maybe Your Own*. San Francisco: Jossey-Bass, 2003.

Bossidy, Larry, and Ram Charan. *Execution: The Discipline of Getting Things Done*. New York: Random House Business Books, 2011.

Brooks, David. *The Social Animal*. New York: Random House, 2011.

Castleberry, Joseph. *Your Deepest Dream*. Colorado Springs, CO: NavPress, 2012.

Clark, Evelyn. *Around the Corporate Campfire: How Great Leaders Use Stories to Inspire Success*. Samamish, WA: C&C Publishers, 2004.

Collins, Jim. *How the Mighty Fall: And Why Some Companies Never Give In*. Jim Collins, 2009.

Collins, Jim, and Jerry Poras. *Built to Last: Successful Habits of Visionary Companies*. New York: HarperBusiness, 2004.

Cosden, Darrel. *The Heavenly Good of Earthly Work*. Grand Rapids: Baker Academic, 2006.

Flaherty, John E. *Peter Drucker: Shaping the Management Mind*. New York: Jossey-Bass, 2002.

Fukuyama, Francis. *Trust: The Social Virtue and the Creation of Prosperity*. New York: Free Press, 1996.

Garber, Steven. *Visions of Vocation: Common Grace for the Common Good*. Downers Grove, IL: InterVarsity Press, 2014.

Gates, Bill. *The Road Ahead*. Rev. ed. New York: Viking Press, 1997.

Guinness, Os. *The Call: Finding and Fulfilling the Central Purpose of Your Life*. Nashville: Word Publishing, 1998.

Hendricks, Bill. *The Person Called You: Why You're Here, Why You Matter & What You Should Do With Your Life*. Chicago: Moody, 2014.

Isaacson, Walter. *Steve Jobs*. New York: Simon & Schuster, 2011.

Keller, Tim. *Counterfeit Gods: The Empty Promises of Money, Sex, and Power, and the Only Hope that Matters*. New York: Riverhead Trade, 2011.

Keller, Tim, with Katheryn Leary Alsdorf. *Every Good Endeavor: Connecting Your Work to God's Work*. New York: Dutton, 2012.

Khaneman, Daniel. *Thinking Fast, and Slow*. New York: Farrar, Straus, and Giroux, 2011.

Lewis, C. S. *The Discarded Image: An Introduction to Medieval and Renaissance Literature*. Reprint, Cambridge: Cambridge University Press, 2012.

Peel, Bill, and Walt Larimore. *Workplace Grace: Becoming a Spiritual Influence at Work*. Longview, TX: LeTourneau, 2014.

Peterson, Eugene. *Practice Resurrection: A Conversation on Growing Up in Christ*. Grand Rapids: Eerdmans, 2010.

Pollard, Bill. *The Tides of Life*. Wheaton, IL: Crossway, 2014.

Sheth, Jagdish. *Self-Destructive Habits of Good Companies*. Philadelphia: Wharton, 2007.

Sherman, Amy L. *Kingdom Calling: Vocational Stewardship for the Common Good*. Downers Grove, IL: InterVarsity Press, 2011.

Sproul, R. C. *Stronger than Steel: The Wayne Alderson Story*. New York: Harper and Row, 1980.

White, Jerry. *The Joseph Road: Choices that Determine Your Destiny*. Colorado Springs: NavPress, 2009.

Willard, Dallas. *Hearing God: Developing a Conversational Relationship with God.* Downers Grove, IL: IVP Books, 2012.

Wright, N. T. *Surprised by Hope: Rethinking Heaven, the Resurrection, and the Mission of the Church.* New York: HarperOne, 2008.

Yung, Hwa. *Bribery and Corruption: Biblical Reflections and Case Studies for the Marketplace in Asia.* Singapore: Graceworks 2010.

NOTES

CHAPTER 2: READY?

1. Gloria Nelund, "Defining Success in the Financial World," *Ethix* 80 (March 2012): www.ethix.org.
2. Joseph Castleberry, *Your Deepest Dream* (Colorado Springs, CO: NavPress, 2012), 12–13.

CHAPTER 3: THE FIRST LEADERSHIP ASSIGNMENT

1. Wayne Alderson, "Valuing People Helps Business," *Ethix* 66 (July 2009): www.ethix.org.

CHAPTER 4: A ROUGH START

1. Guy Kawasaki, "Starting a Business: Answer to Lost Jobs," *Ethix* 72 (October 2010): www.ethix.org.

CHAPTER 5: SEXUAL TEMPTATION

1. Hwa Yung, *Bribery and Corruption: Biblical Reflections and Case Studies for the Marketplace in Asia* (Singapore: Graceworks, 2010), vii.
2. Tim Keller, *Counterfeit Gods: The Empty Promises of Money, Sex, and Power, and the Only Hope that Matters* (New York: Riverhead Trade, 2011), 171.

3. Peter Pace, "The Truth as I Know It," *Ethix* 61 (September 2008): www.ethix.org.

Chapter 6: When Bad Things Happen to Good People

1. Steven J. Bell, "Making Cabinets, Changing the World," *Ethix* 60 (July 2008): www.ethix.org.

Chapter 7: Commitment to the Task

1. Tami Heim, "The Business of Books in a Digital Era," *Ethix* 79 (January 2012): www.ethix.org.
2. Steven J. Bell, "Making Cabinets, Changing the World," *Ethix* 60 (July 2008): www.ethix.org.

Chapter 8: A Glimmer of Hope

1. The Charles F. Dolan Lecture Series 2001, Fairfield University, Fairfield, Connecticut.

Chapter 9: The Opportunity at the Right Time

1. Bill Gates, *The Road Ahead* (New York: Viking Press, 1997 rev. ed.), 22.
2. "The Fruit of the Spirit: Applications to Performance Management," *Christian Business Review* (August 2013), 27–34.

Chapter 11: Office Politics

1. Pete Fox, KIROS speaker, Bellevue, WA, September 2008.

Chapter 12: Bringing Bad News to Authority

1. Sherron Watkins, "Did We Learn the Lessons from Enron?" *Ethix* 53 (May 2007): www.ethix.org.

2. Peter Pace, "The Truth as I Know It," *Ethix* 61 (September 2008): www.ethix.org.

CHAPTER 13: TALKING ABOUT GOD IN THE WORKPLACE

1. Rome Hartman, "Television News in the Digital Age," *Ethix* 78 (November 2011): www.ethix.org.
2. C. William Pollard, "Leading by Serving," *Ethix* 49 (September 2006): www.ethix.org.

CHAPTER 14: STRATEGY

1. John S. Reed, "A View from the Top: Banking, Mergers, Technology & Enron," *Ethix* 22 (March 2002): www.ethix.org.

CHAPTER 15: THE BIG PROMOTION

1. C. William Pollard, "The Awesome Responsibility of Leadership," *The Tides of Life* (Wheaton, IL: Crossway, 2014), 125.
2. Hsieh Fu Hua, "Ownership, Separation of Powers Support Ethical Business," *Ethix* 32 (November 2003): www.ethix.org.
3. Gloria Nelund, "Defining Success in the Financial World," *Ethix* 80 (March 2012): www.ethix.org.

CHAPTER 16: DEALING WITH SUCCESS

1. Gloria Nelund, "Defining Success in the Financial World," *Ethix* 80 (March 2012): www.ethix.org.
2. Marshall N. Carter, "Making Sense of the Financial Mess," *Ethix* 71 (August 2010): www.ethix.org.
3. Roland Martin, "Tiger, You Owe Me Nothing," CNN.com (February 19, 2010).
4. Jim Collins, *How the Mighty Fall: And Why Some Companies Never Give In* (Jim Collins, 2009), 20–21.

CHAPTER 17: EXECUTING THE STRATEGY

1. Larry Bossidy and Ram Charan, *Execution: The Discipline of Getting Things Done* (New York: Random House Business Books, 2011), 11.
2. Jim Collins and Jerry Poras, *Built to Last: Successful Habits of Visionary Companies* (New York: HarperBusiness, 2004).
3. Alan Mulally, "Producing Cars with Passion and Involvement," *Ethix* 70 (July 2010): www.ethix.org.

CHAPTER 18: A TROUBLING CUSTOMER

1. Francis Fukuyama, *Trust: The Social Virtue and the Creation of Prosperity* (New York: Free Press, 1996).

CHAPTER 19: TRANSPARENCY, HONESTY, AND INTEGRITY

1. Hwa Yung, *Bribery and Corruption*, ed. Soo-Inn Tan (Singapore: Graceworks, 2010), 29.
2. David Gill, "Benchmark Ethics: Trust Needs Trustworthy," *Ethix* 26 (November 2002): www.ethix.org.
3. Jack vanHartesvelt, "Hard Choices for the Long Term," *Ethix* 82 (November 2012): www.ethix.org.
4. Donald Flow, "Ethics at Flow Automotive," *Ethix* 34 (March 2004): www.ethix.org.
5. James P. Sinegal, "A Long-Term Business Perspective in a Short-Term World," *Ethix* 28 (March 2003): www.ethix.org.
6. Sherron Watkins, "Did We Learn the Lessons from Enron?" *Ethix* 53 (May 2007): www.ethix.org.

CHAPTER 20: FEAR AND FORGIVENESS

1. John E. Flaherty, *Peter Drucker: Shaping the Management Mind* (New York: Jossey-Bass, 2002).
2. Soichiro Honda, http://www.brainyquote.com/quotes/authors/s/soichiro_honda.html.

3. KOMO news release (August 31, 2006), http://www.komonews. com/news/archive/4172916.html.
4. Brad Tilden, "Keeping an Airline Flying," *Ethix* 84 (May 2013): www.ethix.org.
5. Alan Mulally, "Producing Cars with Passion and Involvement," *Ethix* 70 (July 2010): www.ethix.org.

CHAPTER 21: FAIRNESS AND JUSTICE

1. Beverly Bothel, "Maintaining Ethics in a Downturn: Auto Sales, Real Estate, Home Building," *Ethix* 64 (March 2009): www.ethix.org.

CHAPTER 22: TEMPTATION OF POWER

1. Dennis Bakke, "Creating Real Fun at Work," *Ethix* 35 (May 2004): www.ethix.org.
2. Peter Pace, "The Truth as I Know It," *Ethix* 61 (September 2008): www.ethix.org.

CHAPTER 23: TEMPTATION OF MONEY

1. Guy Kawasaki, "Starting a Business: Answer to Lost Jobs," *Ethix* 72 (October 2010): www.ethix.org.
2. Jeff Van Duzer, "Three Causes of Ethical Lapse in Today's Business," *Ethix* 24 (August 2002).
3. Daniel Kahneman, *Thinking, Fast and Slow* (New York: Farrar, Straus, and Giroux, 2011), 55.
4. Steve Reinemund from an interview with Al Erisman, "Connecting Faith and Corporate Leadership," *Comment* (June 2010).
5. Donald Flow, "Ethics at Flow Automotive," *Ethix* 34 (March 2004): www.ethix.org.
6. Van Duzer.

CHAPTER 24: GLOBALIZATION

1. Prabhu Guptara, "A European Perspective on Globalization," *Ethix* 33 (January 2004): www.ethix.org.

2. Gregory R. Page, "The Ethics of Food—A Corporate Perspective," *Ethix* 69 (April 2010): www.ethix.org.
3. Guptara.
4. Steve Reinemund from an interview with Al Erisman, "Connecting Faith and Corporate Leadership," *Comment* (June 2010).
5. Bonnie Wurzbacher, "Bringing Meaning to Work," *Ethix* 67 (December 2009): www.ethix.org.

CHAPTER 25: DID JOSEPH ULTIMATELY FAIL?

1. Jagdish Sheth, *Self-Destructive Habits of Good Companies* (Philadelphia: Wharton, 2007), 2.
2. Wayne Alderson, "Valuing People Helps Business," *Ethix* 66 (July 2009): www.ethix.org.
3. Perry Bigelow, "Maintaining Ethics in a Downturn: Auto Sales, Real Estate, Home Building," *Ethix* 64 (March 2009): www.ethix.org.
4. Donald Flow, "Maintaining Ethics in a Downturn: Auto Sales, Real Estate, Home Building," *Ethix* 64 (March 2009): www.ethix.org.
5. Darrel Cosden, *The Heavenly Good of Earthly Work* (Grand Rapids: Baker Academic, 2006); N. T. Wright, *Surprised by Hope: Rethinking Heaven, the Resurrection, and the Mission of the Church* (New York: HarperOne, 2008); and Eugene Peterson, *Practice Resurrection: A Conversation on Growing Up in Christ* (Grand Rapids: Eerdmans, 2010).

CHAPTER 26: THE CORPORATE STORY

1. Evelyn Clark, *Around the Corporate Campfire: How Great Leaders Use Stories to Inspire Success* (Samamish, WA: C&C Publishers, 2004).
2. David J. McIntyre Jr., "Protecting Customers, Managing Growth at TriWest," *Ethix* 41 (June 2005): www.ethix.org.
3. Wayne Alderson, "Valuing People Helps Business," *Ethix* 66 (July 2009): www.ethix.org.
4. Ralph Larsen, "Best Practices: Making the Hard Decisions," *Ethix* 53 (June 2007): www.ethix.org.
5. Thomas Kuhn, *The Structures of Scientific Revolutions: 50th Anniversary Edition* (Chicago: University of Chicago Press, 2012).

6. C. S. Lewis, *The Discarded Image: An Introduction to Medieval and Renaissance Literature* (repr. Cambridge: Cambridge University Press, 2012).

7. Gloria Nelund, "Defining Success in the Financial World," *Ethix* 80 (March 2012): www.ethix.org.

8. Dallas Willard, *Hearing God: Developing a Conversational Relationship with God* (Downers Grove, IL: IVP Books, 2012), 35.

Chapter 27: Calling

1. Os Guinness, *The Call: Finding and Fulfilling the Central Purpose of Your Life* (Nashville: Word Publishing, 1998), 31.

2. Guinness, *The Call*; Amy L. Sherman, *Kingdom Calling: Vocational Stewardship for the Common Good* (Downers Grove, IL: InterVarsity Press, 2011); Steven Garber, *Visions of Vocation: Common Grace for the Common Good* (Downers Grove, IL: InterVarsity Press, 2014); "Vocation Overview," Theology of Work Project, http://www.theologyofwork.org/key-topics/vocation-overview-article; and Bill Hendricks, *The Person Called You: Why You're Here, Why You Matter & What You Should Do With Your Life* (Chicago: Moody Publishers, 2014).

3. David Batstone, *Saving the Corporate Soul & (Who Knows) Maybe Your Own* (San Francisco: Jossey-Bass, 2003), 1.

4. Barry Rowan, "Bringing Meaning to Work," *Ethix* 76 (July 2011): www.ethix.org.

5. C. William "Bill" Pollard, "Leading by Serving," *Ethix* 49 (September 2006): www.ethix.org.

6. *Forbes* magazine (August 5, 2006).

7. Donald Flow, "Maintaining Ethics in a Downturn: Auto Sales, Real Estate, Home Building," *Ethix* 64 (March 2009): www.ethix.org.

8. Bonnie Wurzbacher, http://blog.spu.edu/cib/conversations/conversation-with-bonnie-wurzbacher.

9. Wurzbacher.

Chapter 28: Final Reflections

1. David Brooks, *The Social Animal* (New York: Random House, 2011), 87–88.

2. Walter Isaacson, *Steve Jobs* (New York: Simon & Schuster, 2011).

Index of Names and Subjects

Note: Page numbers in *italics* indicate most significant occurrences.